ExamWise
For
MCSE/MCP Exam 70-290
Windows Server 2003 Certification:
Managing and Maintaining a Microsoft
Windows Server 2003 Environment
Second Edition

Download Practice Exam Special Edition provided by BeachFront Quizzer

Author:
Jada Brock-Soldavini, MCSE
with the
TRP Author Certification Success Team

Published by

TotalRecall Publications, Inc.
1103 Middlecreek
Friendswood, TX 77546
281-992-3131

NOTE: THIS BOOK IS GUARANTEED:

See details at www.TotalRecallPress.com

TotalRecall Publications, Inc.
This Book is Sponsored by Beachfront Quizzer, Inc.

The views expressed in this book are solely those of the author, and do not represent the views of any other party or parties.

Printed in United States of America
Printed and bound by Data Duplicators of Houston, Texas
Printed and bound by Lightning Source, Inc. in the USA and UK
Printed and bound by BookSurge, Inc in the USA and around the world

Paper Back
ISBN 1-59095-071-2
UPC 6-43977-03290-4

eBook
ISBN 1-59095-633-8
UPC 6-43977-62290-7

The sponsoring editor is Bruce Moran and the production supervisor is Corby R. Tate.
Author: Jada Brock-Soldavini, MCSE

This publication is not sponsored by, endorsed by, or affiliated with Microsoft, Inc. The Windows® Server 2003®, MCP™, MCSE™, MCSD™, and Microsoft logos are trademarks or registered trademarks of Microsoft, Inc. in the United States and certain other countries. All other trademarks are trademarks of their respective owners. Throughout this book, trademarked names are used. Rather than put a trademark symbol after every occurrence of a trademarked name, we used names in an editorial fashion only and to the benefit of the trademark owner. No intention of infringement on trademarks is intended.

Disclaimer Notice: Judgments as to the suitability of the information herein for purchaser's purposes are necessarily the purchaser's responsibility. BeachFront Quizzer, Inc. and TotalRecall Publications, Inc. extend no warranties, make no representations, and assume no responsibility as to the accuracy or suitability of such information for application to the purchaser's intended purposes or for consequences of its use.

I would like to dedicate this book to my husband Michael and children Alyssa, Daniel and Christian. It is wonderful having you for a family. Thank you for your patience, love and support. I know it has been difficult at times. Also, I would like to extend my love, gratitude, and appreciation to my mother Betty Hite and Grandmother Ruth B. Smith for all of the hard work and sacrifices that were made for me growing up. I would also like to give thanks and appreciation to Alfred and Joan Soldavini who are always there to support me. I could not have done this project without your unwavering love and support. I love you all.

Jada Brock-Soldavini

ExamWise
For
MCSE/MCP Exam 70-290
Windows Server 2003 Certification:

Managing and Maintaining a Microsoft Windows Server 2003 Environment

Second Edition

Jada Brock-Soldavini, MCSE
with the
TRP Author Certification Success Team

About the Author

Jada Brock-Soldavini lives in suburban Atlanta and works for the State of Georgia as a Network Services Administrator. She has co-authored or contributed to other numerous works pertaining to Microsoft Windows technologies. She has an A.S. degree in Computer Information Systems and has been in the Information Technology industry for seven years. She is also married to Michael and the mother of three children Alyssa, Daniel and Christian. In her spare time she enjoys cooking, writing and reading anything that pertains to Network and Security technology.

The TRP Author Certification Success Team

Deborah Timmons

Deborah Timmons is a Microsoft Certified Trainer and Microsoft Certified Systems Engineer. She came into the Microsoft technical field after six years in the adaptive technology field, providing technology and training for persons with disabilities. She is the President and co-owner of Integrator Systems Inc.

Alan Grayson

Alan Grayson has a Masters Degree in Systems Management, is a Microsoft Certified Trainer, a Microsoft Certified Systems Engineer and Microsoft Database Administrator and also holds a dozen other certifications.

Patrick Simpson

Patrick Simpson is a Microsoft MCSE, MCSE +I, MCT and a Novell Master CNE and Master CNI. He has been a Microsoft Certified Trainer for five years and working in the IT industry for approximately 9 years, specializing in network consulting and technical education. Patrick has written numerous certification study aids for both Microsoft Windows 2000 exams and for Novell certification exams.

David Smith

David [Darkcat] Smith is Microsoft Certified Trainer (MCT) and Microsoft Certified Systems Engineer (MCSE). He has been working in the IT industry for approximately 15+ year, specializing in directory services design and administration. He also enjoys planning and implementing large scale rollouts.

Tom McCarty

Tom McCarty is currently an independent trainer, network engineer and consultant. He has worked in the computers and networking environment for 20 years as an administrator, end user support and instructor. Tom has the following certifications; MCSE on Windows NT 4.0, MCP+I, MCDBA, MCT on Windows 2000, and MCSA on Windows Server 2003. Along the way he has gained experience in Exchange 5.5 to 2000 upgrades, SMS 2.0 and NT to Active Directory migrations. In addition to Microsoft certification Ton holds CompTIA A+, Network+ and IT Project+ certifications. I always enjoy seeing the light come on in someone's face when they finally nail down something new.

About the Book

As Microsoft Certified Trainers and practicing IT professionals, we drew on our backgrounds to design this insight manual specifically to help you pass the MCP/MCSE Certification: Managing and Maintaining a Microsoft Windows Server 2003 Environment.

Part of the TotalRecall Insiders Book Series, this manual functions as a "refresher course" by providing short summaries of core exam topics and a pre- and post-assessment quiz for each is heavily illustrated with figures, diagrams and photos. Since it also includes lots of real-world material, you can continue to use this Insight Manual as a ready reference on the job. Primarily this Insight Manual is designed to enhance you knowledge and performance, which will enable you to pass the 70-290 exam as easy as a walk on the beach.

So, if you are already networking with fellow professionals and just want a quick refresher course along with practice questions, this InsidersChoice manual is the book for you. As a bonus for buying it, you get a $20 discount towards an online exam with the popular BeachFront Quizzer. See the last page of the book for details.

Work your way through each Chapter to quickly increase your knowledge on Windows Server 2003 Environment by working at your own pace. Each chapter in this book includes a pre- and post-assessment quiz to measure comprehension of each topic. Written to mimic the real exam, you also get complete answers and explanations plus a detailed scoring summary showing test results at the end of each practice exam. The flexibility of the Beachfront Quizzer test engine is the best engine in the business for self study and practicing for the real exam. The database features over 325 practice questions for the 70-290 exam with four (4) major featured styles: Adaptive testing, Simulated Exams, Flash Cards and the very poplar Study Session option.

Each exam is different, because we randomize the questions and randomize the answers. In a Study Session you can focus on specific objectives/chapters, and get detailed explanations for each question including links to the eBook Chapter for further study.

For further exam practice, you can also pair this manual with TotalRecall's handy Q&A workbook ExamWise for MCP/MCSE Managing and Maintaining a Microsoft Windows Server 2003 Environment Exam 70-290. It uses a unique format of two questions per page, with answers and explanations on the reverse page. It also includes free access to a BeachFront Quizzer online exam.

Why Pay More for your Microsoft Exam?
Save $10 on your Microsoft exam today!
from   http://www.getcertify4less.com

Introduction

They have done it again, only this time it may be closer to being right. Microsoft's Windows Server 2003 in my opinion is hands down better than any of its predecessors (although not perfect, nothing ever is). They have really made this product function as it should in a networking environment. Most of the functions are easy to navigate and configure by using the Microsoft Management Console. I was around the industry when DOS was running desktop machines, Novell 3.xx was king of the hill and Windows 3.11 was around sometimes. Which, in all honesty was not that long ago. But considering what is available today with this release in comparison to 10 years ago, it is an incredible display of innovation and technology. I know that many technology professionals working in the field opted to wait out the Windows NT 4.0 migration to Windows 2000 Server and get their hands on the Windows Server 2003 software. If you are one of these people then I believe once you get into the book and also work this out in your test lab you will find that it was worth the wait. It is always helpful (though not necessary) to go through these study guides and try the settings in a test lab environment. Nothing is worse than applying group policy settings on a domain without first testing them out to see what will happen.

I hope that this book will assist you with the difficult job of taking the exam for 70-290. It is chocked full of information that will make you perform better and smarter in the Windows networking environment. Happy reading, and good luck with your technical endeavors. I hope this guide gives you valuable insight and helps you pass those tough exams.

A Quick overview of the book chapters:

Table of Contents

Exam Information and Resources

Exam News

Exam 70-290 was made available August 14, 2003.

http://www.microsoft.com/traincert/exams/70-290.asp

The course provides a general introductory overview of this task.

You will need to supplement the course with additional lab work.

Audience Profile

The Microsoft Certified Systems Administrator (MCSA) on Windows Server 2003 credential is intended for IT professionals who work in the typically complex computing environment of medium to large companies. An MCSA candidate should have 6 to 12 months of experience administering client and network operating systems in environments that have the following characteristics:

- 250 to 5,000 or more users
- Three or more physical locations
- Three or more domain controllers
- Network services and resources such as messaging, database, file and print, proxy server, firewall, Internet, intranet, remote access and client computer management
- Connectivity requirements such as connecting branch offices and individual users in remote locations to the corporate network and connecting corporate networks to the Internet

Credit Toward Certification

When you pass the Implementing, Managing, and Maintaining a Microsoft® Windows® Server 2003 Environment exam, you achieve Microsoft Certified Professional (MCP) status. You also earn credit toward the following certifications:

- **Core** credit toward Microsoft Certified Systems Administrator (MCSA) on Microsoft Windows Server 2003 certification
- **Core** credit toward Microsoft Certified Systems Engineer (MCSE) on Microsoft Windows Server 2003 certification

Recommended Preparation Tools and Resources

We make a wealth of preparation tools and resources are available to you, including courses, books, practice tests and Microsoft Web sites. When you are ready to prepare for this exam, here's where you could start.

Recommended: Instructor-led Courses for This Exam

- Course 2274: Managing a Microsoft Windows Server 2003 Environment
- Course 2275: Maintaining a Microsoft Windows Server 2003 Environment

Microsoft Online Resources

TechNet: Designed for IT professionals, this site includes How-tos, best practices, downloads, technical chats and much more.

MSDN: The Microsoft Developer Network (MSDN) is a reference for developers, featuring code samples, technical articles, newsgroups, chats and more.

Training & Certification Newsgroups: A newsgroup exists for every Microsoft certification. By participating in the ongoing dialogue, you take advantage of a unique opportunity to exchange ideas with and ask questions of others, including more than 750 Microsoft Most Valuable Professionals (MVPs) worldwide.

TotalRecall Self-Paced Training Products

Practice Tests

BeachFront Quizzer, Inc: www.bfq.com

Web Based Training

www.wbtwise.com

Books and eBooks Training Products

www.totalrecallpress.com

Managing and Maintaining Physical and Logical Devices

The objective of this chapter is to provide the reader with an understanding of the following:

1.1 Manage basic disks and dynamic disks

1.2 Monitor server hardware

    1.2.1 Tools used to manage hardware
    1.2.2 Device Manager
    1.2.3 The Hardware Troubleshooting Wizard
    1.2.4 Appropriate Control Panel items

1.3 Optimize server disk performance

    1.2.1 Implement a RAID solution
    1.2.2 Defragment volumes and partitions

1.4 Troubleshoot server hardware devices

    1.4 1 Diagnose and resolve issues related to hardware settings
    1.4 2 Diagnose and resolve issues related to server hardware
    1.4 3 Diagnose and resolve issues related to hardware driver upgrades

1.5 Install and configure server hardware devices

    1.5.1 Configure driver signing options
    1.5.2 Configure resource settings for a device
    1.5.3 Configure device properties and settings

Chapter 1: Physical & Logical Devices

1. (QID 1) You decide to create a logical volume on your Server 2003 machine using Disk Management. How can you accomplish this?

   A. Go into Control Panel and select Computer Management. Right-click free space on an extended partition where you want to create the logical drive, and then click New Logical Drive. Use the New Partition wizard.

   B. Go into Control Panel and select Disk Management. Right-click free space on an extended partition where you want to create the logical drive, and then click New Logical Drive. Use the New Partition wizard.

   C. Go into Computer Management and select Disk Management. Right-click free space on an extended partition where you want to create the logical drive, and then click New Logical Drive. Use the New Partition wizard.

   D. Go into Computer Management and select Disk Management. Right-click used space on an extended partition where you want to create the logical drive, and then click New Logical Drive. Use the New Partition wizard.

---

2. (QID 2) How can you format a partition with Disk Management?

   A. Right-click the partition or logical drive that you want to format, and then click Format.

   B. Right-click the disk that you want to format, and then click Format.

   C. Right-click Removable Storage, and then click Format.

   D. Right-click Shared Folders, and then click Format.

1. (QID 1) You decide to create a logical volume on your Server 2003 machine using Disk Management. How can you accomplish this?

    A. Go into Control Panel and select Computer Management. Right-click free space on an extended partition where you want to create the logical drive, and then click New Logical Drive. Use the New Partition wizard.

    B. Go into Control Panel and select Disk Management. Right-click free space on an extended partition where you want to create the logical drive, and then click New Logical Drive. Use the New Partition wizard.

***C. Go into Computer Management and select Disk Management. Right-click free space on an extended partition where you want to create the logical drive, and then click New Logical Drive. Use the New Partition wizard.**

    D. Go into Computer Management and select Disk Management. Right-click used space on an extended partition where you want to create the logical drive, and then click New Logical Drive. Use the New Partition wizard.

Explanation: To create a new partition or logical drive, select the Disk Management option in Computer Management. To create a new partition, right-click unallocated space on the basic disk where you want to create the partition, and then click New Partition. You can also right-click free space on an extended partition where you want to create the logical drive, and then click New Logical Drive. On the Welcome to the New Partition Wizard page, click Next. On the Select Partition Type page, click the type of partition that you want to create, and then click Next. On the Specify Partition Size page, specify the size in megabytes (MB) of the partition that you want to create, and then click Next. On the Assign Drive Letter or Path page, enter a drive letter or drive path, and then click Next. On the Format Partition page, specify the formatting options that you want, and then click Next. On the Completing the New Partition Wizard page, verify that the options that you selected are correct, and then click Finish.

---

2. (QID 2) How can you format a partition with Disk Management?

***A. Right-click the partition or logical drive that you want to format, and then click Format.**

    B. Right-click the disk that you want to format, and then click Format.

    C. Right-click Removable Storage, and then click Format.

    D. Right-click Shared Folders, and then click Format.

Explanation: If you want to format a partition, In the Disk Management window, right-click the partition or logical drive that you want to format, and then click Format. Specify the formatting options that you want, and then click OK. Click OK when you are prompted to confirm the formatting changes.

3. (QID 3) How do you convert a basic disk into a dynamic disk in Windows 2003?

    A. Select Removable Media

    B. Right-click the basic disk

    C. Click Convert to Dynamic Disk

    D. Select Shared Folders

    E. Select Disk Management

---

4. (QID 4) You want to create a simple volume on your Server 2003 machine. Which of the following steps are necessary?

    A. Select New Simple Volume

    B. Select unallocated space on a dynamic disk

    C. Select New Volume

    D. Select unallocated space on a basic disk

    E. In Computer Management, select Disk Management.

3. (QID 3) How do you convert a basic disk into a dynamic disk in Windows 2003?

    A. Select Removable Media

***B. Right-click the basic disk**

***C. Click Convert to Dynamic Disk**

    D. Select Shared Folders

***E. Select Disk Management**

Explanation: In the graphical view of the Disk Management window, right-click the basic disk that you want to change, and then click Convert to Dynamic Disk. Click to select the check box next to the disk that you want to change, and then click OK. If you want to view the list of volumes in the disk, click Details in the Disks to Convert dialog box. Click Convert. Click Yes when you are prompted to confirm the conversion, and then click OK.

---

4. (QID 4) You want to create a simple volume on your Server 2003 machine. Which of the following steps are necessary?

    A. Select New Simple Volume

***B. Select unallocated space on a dynamic disk**

***C. Select New Volume**

    D. Select unallocated space on a basic disk

***E. In Computer Management, select Disk Management.**

Explanation: To create a simple volume, go to Computer Management and select Disk Management. Right-click unallocated space on the dynamic disk where you want to create the simple volume, and then click New Volume. You can also create a spanned volume by right-clicking unallocated space on the dynamic disk where you want to create the spanned volume, and then click New Volume. On the Welcome to the New Volume Wizard page, click Next. On the Select Volume Type page, click either Simple volume or Spanned volume, and then click Next.

On the Select Disks page, if you are creating a simple volume, verify that the disk, on which you want to create a simple volume, is listed in the Selected dynamic disks box. If you are creating a spanned volume, click to select the disks that you want under All available dynamic disks, and then click Add. Verify that the disks, on which you want to create a spanned volume, are listed in the Selected dynamic disks box. In the Size box, specify the size (in MB) that you want for the volume, and then click Next. On the Assign Drive Letter or Path page, enter a drive letter or drive path, and then click Next. On the Format Volume page, specify the formatting options that you want, and then click Next. On the Completing the New Volume Wizard page, make sure that the options that you selected are correct, and then click Finish.

5. (QID 5) You want to create a spanned volume on your Server 2003 machine. Which of the following steps are necessary?

    A. In Computer Management, select Disk Management.

    B. Select New Spanned Volume

    C. Select New Volume

    D. Select unallocated space on a basic disk

    E. Select unallocated space on a dynamic disk

---

7. (QID 7) Which of the following status indicators do not require repairs?

    A. Offline

    B. Healthy

    C. Online with errors

    D. Online

    E. Missing

5. (QID 5) You want to create a spanned volume on your Server 2003 machine. Which of the following steps are necessary?

***A. In Computer Management, select Disk Management.**

    B. Select New Spanned Volume

***C. Select New Volume**

    D. Select unallocated space on a basic disk

***E. Select unallocated space on a dynamic disk**

Explanation: To create a simple volume, go to Computer Management and select Disk Management. Right-click unallocated space on the dynamic disk where you want to create the simple volume, and then click New Volume. You can also create a spanned volume by right-clicking unallocated space on the dynamic disk where you want to create the spanned volume, and then click New Volume. On the Welcome to the New Volume Wizard page, click Next. On the Select Volume Type page, click either Simple volume or Spanned volume, and then click Next.

On the Select Disks page, if you are creating a simple volume, verify that the disk on which you want to create a simple volume is listed in the Selected dynamic disks box. If you are creating a spanned volume, click to select the disks that you want under All available dynamic disks, and then click Add. Verify that the disks on which you want to create a spanned volume are listed in the Selected dynamic disks box. In the Size box, specify the size (in MB) that you want for the volume, and then click Next. On the Assign Drive Letter or Path page, enter a drive letter or drive path, and then click Next. On the Format Volume page, specify the formatting options that you want, and then click Next. On the Completing the New Volume Wizard page, make sure that the options that you selected are correct, and then click Finish.

---

6. (QID 6) Which of the following status indicators do not require repairs?

    A. Offline

***B. Healthy**

    C. Online with errors

***D. Online**

    E. Missing

Explanation: When a disk or volume fails, Disk Management displays status descriptions of disks and volumes in the Disk Management window. These descriptions, are as follows: Online, Healthy (either of these are normal), Online with errors (indicative of I/O errors on a dynamic disk - to resolve this issue, right-click the disk, and then click Reactivate Disk to return the disk to regular Online status), Offline or Missing (displayed when dynamic disks are corrupted, inaccessible, or temporarily unavailable - to resolve this issue, repair any disk, controller, or connection problems, verify that the physical disk is turned on and correctly attached to the computer, right-click the disk, and then click Reactivate Disk to return the disk to Online status).

7. (QID 7) Which of the following are things you have to indicate when creating a spanned volume?

A. Disks used

B. RAM use

C. The format used

D. The size of the volume

E. Type of hard disk used

---

8. (QID 8) Which of the following status indicators require repair or troubleshooting?

A. Online

B. Missing

C. Offline

D. Online with errors

E. Healthy

7. (QID 7) Which of the following are things you have to indicate when creating a spanned volume?

***A. Disks used**

    B. RAM use

***C. The format used**

***D. The size of the volume**

    E. Type of hard disk used

Explanation: To create a simple volume, go to Computer Management and select Disk Management. Right-click unallocated space on the dynamic disk where you want to create the simple volume, and then click New Volume. You can also create a spanned volume by right-clicking unallocated space on the dynamic disk where you want to create the spanned volume, and then click New Volume. On the Welcome to the New Volume Wizard page, click Next. On the Select Volume Type page, click either Simple volume or Spanned volume, and then click Next.

On the Select Disks page, if you are creating a simple volume, verify that the disk on which you want to create a simple volume is listed in the Selected dynamic disks box. If you are creating a spanned volume, click to select the disks that you want under All available dynamic disks, and then click Add. Verify that the disks on which you want to create a spanned volume are listed in the Selected dynamic disks box. In the Size box, specify the size (in MB) that you want for the volume, and then click Next. On the Assign Drive Letter or Path page, enter a drive letter or drive path, and then click Next. On the Format Volume page, specify the formatting options that you want, and then click Next. On the Completing the New Volume Wizard page, make sure that the options that you selected are correct, and then click Finish.

---

8. (QID 8) Which of the following status indicators require repair or troubleshooting?

    A. Online

***B. Missing**

***C. Offline**

***D. Online with errors**

    E. Healthy

Explanation: When a disk or volume fails, Disk Management displays status descriptions of disks and volumes in the Disk Management window. These descriptions, are as follows: Online, Healthy (either of these is normal), Online with errors (indicative of I/O errors on a dynamic disk - to resolve this issue, right-click the disk, and then click Reactivate Disk to return the disk to regular Online status), Offline or Missing (displayed when dynamic disks are corrupted, inaccessible, or temporarily unavailable - to resolve this issue, repair any disk, controller, or connection problems, verify that the physical disk is turned on and correctly attached to the computer, right-click the disk, and then click Reactivate Disk to return the disk to Online status).

9. (QID 9) You attempt to access your G: drive, but you find that the status of the G: drive is offline with errors. What action should you take to change the status of the G: drive to online?

A. Double-click the disk, and then click Reactivate Disk to return the disk to regular Online status.

B. Right-click the disk, and then click Reactivate Disk to return the disk to regular Online status.

C. Right-click the disk, and then click Enable Disk to return the disk to regular Online status.

D. Double-click the disk, and then click Enable Disk to return the disk to regular Online status.

---

10. (QID 10) You attempt to access your H: drive, but you find that the status of the H: drive is missing. What action should you take to change the status of the H: drive to online?

A. Check for problems with the hard disk

B. Partition the disk

C. Reactivate the disk to Online status

D. Reformat the disk

E. Verify that the physical disk is correctly attached to the computer

9. (QID 9) You attempt to access your G: drive, but you find that the status of the G: drive is offline with errors. What action should you take to change the status of the G: drive to online?

    A. Double-click the disk, and then click Reactivate Disk to return the disk to regular Online status.

***B. Right-click the disk, and then click Reactivate Disk to return the disk to regular Online status.**

    C. Right-click the disk, and then click Enable Disk to return the disk to regular Online status.

    D. Double-click the disk, and then click Enable Disk to return the disk to regular Online status.

Explanation: When a disk or volume fails, Disk Management displays status descriptions of disks and volumes in the Disk Management window. These descriptions, are as follows: Online, Healthy (either of these are normal), Online with errors (indicative of I/O errors on a dynamic disk - to resolve this issue, right-click the disk, and then click Reactivate Disk to return the disk to regular Online status), Offline or Missing (displayed when dynamic disks are corrupted, inaccessible, or temporarily unavailable - to resolve this issue, repair any disk, controller, or connection problems, verify that the physical disk is turned on and correctly attached to the computer, right-click the disk, and then click Reactivate Disk to return the disk to Online status).

---

10. (QID 10) You attempt to access your H: drive, but you find that the status of the H: drive is missing. What action should you take to change the status of the H: drive to online?

***A. Check for problems with the hard disk**

    B. Partition the disk

***C. Reactivate the disk to Online status**

    D. Reformat the disk

***E. Verify that the physical disk is correctly attached to the computer**

Explanation: When a disk or volume fails, Disk Management displays status descriptions of disks and volumes in the Disk Management window. These descriptions, are as follows: Online, Healthy (either of these is normal), Online with errors (indicative of I/O errors on a dynamic disk - to resolve this issue, right-click the disk, and then click Reactivate Disk to return the disk to regular Online status), Offline or Missing (displayed when dynamic disks are corrupted, inaccessible, or temporarily unavailable - to resolve this issue, repair any disk, controller, or connection problems, verify that the physical disk is turned on and correctly attached to the computer, right-click the disk, and then click Reactivate Disk to return the disk to Online status).

11. (QID 11) You want to manually configure the IRQ on a newly installed piece of hardware. What steps do you need to take to accomplish this in Device Manager?

    A. Right-click the device that you want to configure, and then click Properties.

    B. Click the Resources tab and click to clear the Use automatic settings check box.

    C. Click the Advanced tab and click to clear the Use automatic settings check box.

    D. Click the General tab and click to clear the Use automatic settings check box.

    E. In the Settings based on box, click the hardware configuration that you want to modify and under Resource type in the Resource settings box, click the type of resource that you want to modify. Click Change Setting. In the Edit Resource dialog box, type the value that you want for the resource, and then click OK.

---

12. (QID 12) You suspect that there may be a device conflict in your 2003 Server machine. How can you use Device Manager to determine if this is the case?

    A. Right-click the device that you want to test for conflicts, and then click Properties. Click the Resources tab. Any conflicts that exist for the device are listed under Conflicting device list.

    B. Double-click the device that you want to test for conflicts, and then click Properties. Click the Resources tab. Any conflicts that exist for the device are listed under Conflicting device list.

    C. Right-click the device that you want to test for conflicts, and then click Properties. Click the General tab. Any conflicts that exist for the device are listed under Conflicting device list.

    D. Right-click the device that you want to test for conflicts, and then click Properties. Click the Advanced tab. Any conflicts that exist for the device are listed under Conflicting device list.

11. (QID 11) You want to manually configure the IRQ on a newly installed piece of hardware. What steps do you need to take to accomplish this in Device Manager?

***A. Right-click the device that you want to configure, and then click Properties.**
***B. Click the Resources tab and click to clear the Use automatic settings check box.**
    C. Click the Advanced tab and click to clear the Use automatic settings check box.
    D. Click the General tab and click to clear the Use automatic settings check box.
***E. In the Settings based on box, click the hardware configuration that you want to modify and under Resource type in the Resource settings box, click the type of resource that you want to modify. Click Change Setting. In the Edit Resource dialog box, type the value that you want for the resource, and then click OK.**

Explanation: To configure a device in Device Manager, Click Start, point to Administrative Tools, and then click Computer Management. Under System Tools in the console tree, click Device Manager. Double-click the type of device that you want to configure. Right-click the device that you want to configure, and then click Properties. Click the Resources tab. Click to clear the Use automatic settings check box. In the Settings based on box, click the hardware configuration that you want to modify (i.e. - Basic configuration 0000). Under Resource type in the Resource settings box, click the type of resource that you want to modify (i.e. - Interrupt Request). Click Change Setting. In the Edit Resource dialog box, type the value that you want for the resource, and then click OK.

---

12. (QID 12) You suspect that there may be a device conflict in your 2003 Server machine. How can you use Device Manager to determine if this is the case?

***A. Right-click the device that you want to test for conflicts, and then click Properties. Click the Resources tab. Any conflicts that exist for the device are listed under Conflicting device list.**
    B. Double-click the device that you want to test for conflicts, and then click Properties. Click the Resources tab. Any conflicts that exist for the device are listed under Conflicting device list.
    C. Right-click the device that you want to test for conflicts, and then click Properties. Click the General tab. Any conflicts that exist for the device are listed under Conflicting device list.
    D. Right-click the device that you want to test for conflicts, and then click Properties. Click the Advanced tab. Any conflicts that exist for the device are listed under Conflicting device list.

Explanation: If you want to search for device conflicts, click Start, point to Administrative Tools, and then click Computer Management. Under System Tools in the console tree, click Device Manager. Double-click the type of device that you want to test. Right-click the device that you want to test for conflicts, and then click Properties. Click the Resources tab. Any conflicts that exist for the device are listed under Conflicting device list.

13. (QID 13) You want to resolve a hardware conflict on your 2003 Server machine. What actions should you take?

A. In Device manager, right-click the device that you want to troubleshoot, and then click Properties. Click the General tab. Click Test.

B. In Device manager, right-click the device that you want to troubleshoot, and then click Properties. Click the Advanced tab. Click Troubleshoot.

C. In Device manager, right-click the device that you want to troubleshoot, and then click Properties. Click the Resources tab. Click Troubleshoot.

D. In Device manager, right-click the device that you want to troubleshoot, and then click Properties. Click the General tab. Click Troubleshoot.

13. (QID 13) You want to resolve a hardware conflict on your 2003 Server machine. What actions should you take?

>   A. In Device manager, right-click the device that you want to troubleshoot, and then click Properties. Click the General tab. Click Test.
>   B. In Device manager, right-click the device that you want to troubleshoot, and then click Properties. Click the Advanced tab. Click Troubleshoot.
>   C. In Device manager, right-click the device that you want to troubleshoot, and then click Properties. Click the Resources tab. Click Troubleshoot.

***D. In Device manager, right-click the device that you want to troubleshoot, and then click Properties. Click the General tab. Click Troubleshoot.**

Explanation: To start the Windows Hardware Troubleshooter, Click Start, point to Administrative Tools, and then click Computer Management. Under System Tools in the console tree, click Device Manager. Double-click the type of device that you want to troubleshoot. Right-click the device that you want to troubleshoot, and then click Properties. Click the General tab. Click Troubleshoot.

14. (QID 14) The CIO of your company wants you to build a RAID array that will continue to function even after one of the drives in the array fails. You recommend to the CIO that a software version of RAID 5 is available in Windows 2003. How would you set this up?

A. In Disk Management, right-click the unallocated space on one of the dynamic disks where you want to create the RAID-5 volume, and then click Create Volume.

B. After the Create Volume Wizard starts, click Next. Click RAID-5 volume, and then click Next. Click the disks in the left pane under All Available Dynamic Disks, and then click the Add tab. Look at the bottom of the Select Disk dialog box under the Size label. The For All Selected Disks box displays the maximum size of the RAID-5 volume that you can make. Click Next.

C. Click Assign Drive Letter, and then enter an available drive letter. Click Next. Click Format this partition with the following settings, and select the file system type (FAT32 or NTFS). Leave the default selection in the Allocation Unit Size box. In the Volume Label box, you can keep the default 'New Volume' label or you can type your own label. At this time, you can click to select the Quick Format check box and the File and Folder Compression check box. Click Next, check your selection in the Summary window, and then click Finish.

D. Run low-level formatting and click next.

E. Run hyper-formatting and click next.

14. (QID 14) The CIO of your company wants you to build a RAID array that will continue to function even after one of the drives in the array fails. You recommend to the CIO that a software version of RAID 5 is available in Windows 2003. How would you set this up?

***A. In Disk Management, right-click the unallocated space on one of the dynamic disks where you want to create the RAID-5 volume, and then click Create Volume.**
***B. After the Create Volume Wizard starts, click Next. Click RAID-5 volume, and then click Next. Click the disks in the left pane under All Available Dynamic Disks, and then click the Add tab. Look at the bottom of the Select Disk dialog box under the Size label. The For All Selected Disks box displays the maximum size of the RAID-5 volume that you can make. Click Next.**
***C. Click Assign Drive Letter, and then enter an available drive letter. Click Next. Click Format this partition with the following settings, and select the file system type (FAT32 or NTFS). Leave the default selection in the Allocation Unit Size box. In the Volume Label box, you can keep the default 'New Volume' label or you can type your own label. At this time, you can click to select the Quick Format check box and the File and Folder Compression check box. Click Next, check your selection in the Summary window, and then click Finish.**
  D. Run low-level formatting and click next.
  E. Run hyper-formatting and click next.

Explanation: In the Disk Management tool, right-click the unallocated space on one of the dynamic disks where you want to create the RAID-5 volume, and then click Create Volume. After the Create Volume Wizard starts, click Next. Click RAID-5 volume, and then click Next. Click the disks in the left pane under All Available Dynamic Disks, and then click the Add tab. Look at the bottom of the Select Disk dialog box under the Size label. The For All Selected Disks box displays the maximum size of the RAID-5 volume that you can make. Click Next.

At this time, you may want to assign a drive letter (you can also do this at any other time). To do so, click Assign Drive Letter, and then enter an available drive letter. Alternatively, you can click Do not assign drive letter or path. Click Next. Click Format this partition with the following settings, and select the file system type (FAT32 or NTFS). Leave the default selection in the Allocation Unit Size box. In the Volume Label box, you can keep the default 'New Volume' label or you can type your own label. At this time, you can click to select the Quick Format check box and the File and Folder Compression check box. Click Next, check your selection in the Summary window, and then click Finish.

15. (QID 15) One of your engineers want to create a RAID 5 array on one of the 2003 servers on your network, but informs you that the server on which he plans to set up the RAID array may not meet minimum requirements. What should you instruct him to check to ensure that the RAID 5 array can be created?

    A. You need at least three drives

    B. All disks must be dynamic

    C. Disks can be either basic or dynamic

    D. You need two drives

    E. IDE, EIDE, and SCSI drives can all be used together

---

16. (QID 16) Which colored region should be reduced when analyzing files using Disk Defragmenter?

    A. Purple

    B. Blue

    C. Green

    D. Yellow

    E. Red

15. (QID 15) One of your engineers want to create a RAID 5 array on one of the 2003 servers on your network, but informs you that the server on which he plans to set up the RAID array may not meet minimum requirements. What should you instruct him to check to ensure that the RAID 5 array can be created?

***A. You need at least three drives**
***B. All disks must be dynamic**
    C. Disks can be either basic or dynamic
    D. You need two drives   .
***E. IDE, EIDE, and SCSI drives can all be used together**

Explanation: When setting up RAID 5, you must have a minimum of three disks to support striping. All disks involved in striping must be dynamic. The RAID-5 volume can take the whole disk or as little as 20 megabytes (MB) for each disk. Any disks that you want to upgrade to a dynamic disk must contain at least 1 MB of free space at the end of the disk for the upgrade to succeed. The status of all disks involved in a stripe volume must be online when you create the striped volume. IDE, EIDE, and SCSI drives can all be used in one stripe volume.

---

16. (QID 16) Which colored region should be reduced when analyzing files using Disk Defragmenter?

    A. Purple
    B. Blue
    C. Green
    D. Yellow
***E. Red**

Explanation: If you want to defragment a disk volume, click Start, point to All Programs, point to Accessories, point to System Tools, and then click Disk Defragmenter. Select the volume that you want to defragment. Click Defragment to start the operation. Review the progress of the operation in the Estimated disk usage before fragmentation and Estimated disk usage after fragmentation windows. Defragmented files on the disk appear in red, contiguous files in blue, and system files in green. The goal is to get rid of most of the red in the Estimated disk usage before fragmentation window. After the analysis is complete, click View Report in the Disk Defragmenter dialog box to review the results of the disk defragmentation.

17. (QID 17) When using Disk Defragmenter, which color represents contiguous files?

    A. Blue

    B. Red

    C. Green

    D. Yellow

    E. Purple

---

18. (QID 18) Which of the following is the correct path to start Disk Defragmenter in Windows 2003?

    A. Click Start, point to All Programs, point to Administrative Tools, point to System Tools, and then click Disk Defragmenter.

    B. Click Start, point to All Programs, point to Accessories, point to System Tools, and then click Disk Defragmenter.

    C. Click Start, point to All Programs, point to Administrative Tools, point to Computer Management, and then click Disk Defragmenter.

    D. Click Start, point to All Programs, point to Accessories, point to Computer Management, and then click Disk Defragmenter.

17. (QID 17) When using Disk Defragmenter, which color represents contiguous files?
*A. Blue
    B. Red
    C. Green
    D. Yellow
    E. Purple

Explanation: If you want to defragment a disk volume, click Start, point to All Programs, point to Accessories, point to System Tools, and then click Disk Defragmenter. Select the volume that you want to defragment. Click Defragment to start the operation. Review the progress of the operation in the Estimated disk usage before fragmentation and Estimated disk usage after fragmentation windows. Defragmented files on the disk appear in red, contiguous files in blue, and system files in green. The goal is to get rid of most of the red in the Estimated disk usage before fragmentation window. After the analysis is complete, click View Report in the Disk Defragmenter dialog box to review the results of the disk defragmentation.

---

18. (QID 18) Which of the following is the correct path to start Disk Defragmenter in Windows 2003?

    A. Click Start, point to All Programs, point to Administrative Tools, point to System Tools, and then click Disk Defragmenter.

***B. Click Start, point to All Programs, point to Accessories, point to System Tools, and then click Disk Defragmenter.**

    C. Click Start, point to All Programs, point to Administrative Tools, point to Computer Management, and then click Disk Defragmenter.

    D. Click Start, point to All Programs, point to Accessories, point to Computer Management, and then click Disk Defragmenter.

Explanation: If you want to defragment a disk volume, click Start, point to All Programs, point to Accessories, point to System Tools, and then click Disk Defragmenter. Select the volume that you want to defragment. Click Defragment to start the operation. Review the progress of the operation in the Estimated disk usage before fragmentation and Estimated disk usage after fragmentation windows. Defragmented files on the disk appear in red, contiguous files in blue, and system files in green. The goal is to get rid of most of the red in the Estimated disk usage before fragmentation window. After the analysis is complete, click View Report in the Disk Defragmenter dialog box to review the results of the disk defragmentation.

19. (QID 19) You want to make sure that the junior network associates install only Microsoft signed drivers on the 2003 server that handles file and print services for the network. How can you do this?

    A. In System properties, select the hardware tab. Click the driver signing button. Set the driver signing option to kill when you attempt to install.

    B. In System properties, select the hardware tab. Click the driver signing button. Set the driver signing option to ignore when you attempt to install unsigned drivers.

    C. In System properties, select the hardware tab. Click the driver signing button. Set the driver signing option to warn when you attempt to install unsigned drivers.

    D. In System properties, select the hardware tab. Click the driver signing button. Set the driver signing option to block when you attempt to install unsigned drivers.unsigned drivers.

20. (QID 20) Which of the following situations with a NIC card could produce a bottleneck?

    A. An unplugged NIC card

    B. A NIC card that is set for 10 Mbps when it should be set to 100 Mbps

    C. An older network card that is installed on a new server

    D. A fibre channel NIC

19. (QID 19) You want to make sure that the junior network associates install only Microsoft signed drivers on the 2003 server that handles file and print services for the network. How can you do this?

A. In System properties, select the hardware tab. Click the driver signing button. Set the driver signing option to kill when you attempt to install.

B. In System properties, select the hardware tab. Click the driver signing button. Set the driver signing option to ignore when you attempt to install unsigned drivers.

C. In System properties, select the hardware tab. Click the driver signing button. Set the driver signing option to warn when you attempt to install unsigned drivers.

***D. In System properties, select the hardware tab. Click the driver signing button. Set the driver signing option to block when you attempt to install unsigned drivers.unsigned drivers.**

Explanation: In System properties, select the hardware tab. Click the driver signing button. Set the driver signing option to ignore, warn or block when you attempt to install unsigned drivers.

20. (QID 20) Which of the following situations with a NIC card could produce a bottleneck?

A. An unplugged NIC card

***B. A NIC card that is set for 10 Mbps when it should be set to 100 Mbps**

***C. An older network card that is installed on a new server**

D. A fibre channel NIC

Explanation: Lack of memory is a major cause of bottlenecks. An older network card that is installed on a new server may cause a bottleneck. A failing hard drive may cause a bottleneck. A program that monopolizes a particular resource can be a bootleneck. An older multispeed network card may be configured for 10 megabits per second (Mbps) when it should be set to 100 Mbps and this would produce a bottleneck.

21. (QID 21) Which of the following scenarios could result in a bottleneck?

    A. Two hard drive controllers

    B. Too much physical memory

    C. A program set to low priority

    D. A new hard drive

    E. Not enough physical memory

---

22. (QID 22) You want to perform real-time monitoring on your Windows 2003 Server. Which of the following methods will allow you to do this?

    A. Click Start, point to Administrative Tools, and then click Performance.

    B. Open a command prompt window or the Run box and type perfmon.exe

    C. Click Start, point to Programs, and then click Performance.

    D. Open a command prompt window or the Run box and type perfmon.msc

21. (QID 21) Which of the following scenarios could result in a bottleneck?

    A. Two hard drive controllers
    B. Too much physical memory
    C. A program set to low priority
    D. A new hard drive

***E. Not enough physical memory**

Explanation: Lack of memory is a major cause of bottlenecks. An older network card that is installed on a new server may cause a bottleneck. A failing hard drive may cause a bottleneck. A program that monopolizes a particular resource can be a bootleneck. An older multispeed network card may be configured for 10 megabits per second (Mbps) when it should be set to 100 Mbps and this would produce a bottleneck.

---

22. (QID 22) You want to perform real-time monitoring on your Windows 2003 Server. Which of the following methods will allow you to do this?

***A. Click Start, point to Administrative Tools, and then click Performance.**
    B. Open a command prompt window or the Run box and type perfmon.exe
    C. Click Start, point to Programs, and then click Performance.

***D. Open a command prompt window or the Run box and type perfmon.msc**

Explanation: To start Performance, click Start, point to Administrative Tools, and then click Performance. You can also start Performance by opening a command prompt window and typing perfmon.msc.

23. (QID 23) Which of the following can you manage with the Diskpart command?

    A. Disks

    B. Physical memory

    C. Volumes

    D. Virtual memory

    E. Partitions

---

24. (QID 24) Which of the following statements are true in regards to logical drives in Windows 2003?

    A. You can have up to 14 of them

    B. You can have up to 4 of them

    C. You can have up to 24 of them

    D. You can assign a drive letter to them

    E. You cannot assign a drive letter to them

23. (QID 23) Which of the following can you manage with the Diskpart command?

***A. Disks**

    B. Physical memory

***C. Volumes**

    D. Virtual memory

***E. Partitions**

Explanation: By using the DiskPart command-line tool, you can perform many disk management tasks from the command line. Use DiskPart to perform disk-related tasks at the command line as an alternative to using Disk Management. DiskPart is a text-mode command interpreter that enables you to manage objects, such as disks, partitions, and volumes, by using scripts or direct input from a command prompt. Administrators often write scripts to perform repetitive tasks.

---

24. (QID 24) Which of the following statements are true in regards to logical drives in Windows 2003?

    A. You can have up to 14 of them

    B. You can have up to 4 of them

***C. You can have up to 24 of them**

***D. You can assign a drive letter to them**

    E. You cannot assign a drive letter to them

Explanation: In Windows 2003, you can create up to 24 logical drives per disk but are limited to four primary partitions per disk. You can format a logical drive and assign a drive letter to it.

25. (QID 25) Which of the following statements about deleting partitions in Windows 2003 are true?

   A. It preserves all of the data in the partition

   B. It changes the space used by the partition to unallocated space

   C. It destroys all of the data in the partition

   D. It does not changes the space used by the partition to unallocated space

---

26. (QID 26) Select the appropriate steps when creating a 5 GB primary partition on your first hard disk with the DISKPART command?

   A. From a command-line, type diskpart, then list disk.

   B. From a command-line, type diskpart, then read disk.

   C. At the DISKPART prompt, type select disk 1, and type create partition primary size=50

   D. At the DISKPART prompt, type select disk 0, and type create partition primary size=5000

   E. At the DISKPART prompt, type select disk 1, and type create partition primary size=500

25. (QID 25) Which of the following statements about deleting partitions in Windows 2003 are true?

    A. It preserves all of the data in the partition

***B. It changes the space used by the partition to unallocated space**

***C. It destroys all of the data in the partition**

    D. It does not changes the space used by the partition to unallocated space

Explanation: Deleting a partition destroys all of the data in the partition and changes the space used by the partition to unallocated space. If it is an extended partition, you must delete all of its logical drives on the disk before deleting the partition.

---

26. (QID 26) Select the appropriate steps when creating a 5 GB primary partition on your first hard disk with the DISKPART command?

***A. From a command-line, type diskpart, then list disk.**

    B. From a command-line, type diskpart, then read disk.

    C. At the DISKPART prompt, type select disk 1, and type create partition primary size=50

***D. At the DISKPART prompt, type select disk 0, and type create partition primary size=5000**

    E. At the DISKPART prompt, type select disk 1, and type create partition primary size=500

Explanation: To partition a disk by using DiskPart, type diskpart from a command-line. At the prompt, type 'list disk' and then make a note of the number of the disks on which you want to create a primary or extended partition. At the DISKPART prompt, type 'select disk n' (where n is the disk number of the disk where you want to create the primary or extended partition). At the DISKPART prompt, type one of the following (where number is in megabytes): create partition primary size=number, create partition extended size=number, or create partition logical size=number

27. (QID 27) How can you view what type of disk you have using the DISKPART command?

    A. From a command-line, type detail disk.

    B. From a command-line, type select disk 0, and then detail disk.

    C. From a command-line, type diskpart, and then detail disk.

    D. From a command-line, type memory disk.

    E. From a command-line, type diskpart, then select disk 0, and then detail disk.

28. (QID 28) Which of the following commands, when typed from a DISKPART command, will convert a disk to a dynamic disk?

    A. convert dynamic

    B. convert dyn

    C. change dynamic

    D. dynamic

27. (QID 27) How can you view what type of disk you have using the DISKPART command?

    A. From a command-line, type detail disk.
    B. From a command-line, type select disk 0, and then detail disk.
    C. From a command-line, type diskpart, and then detail disk.
    D. From a command-line, type memory disk.
***E. From a command-line, type diskpart, then select disk 0, and then detail disk.**

Explanation: To view the disk type by using DiskPart, open a command prompt. Type the following commands at the prompt, pressing ENTER after each command: 'diskpart', 'select disk 0', and 'detail disk'.

---

28. (QID 28) Which of the following commands, when typed from a DISKPART command, will convert a disk to a dynamic disk?

***A. convert dynamic**
    B. convert dyn
    C. change dynamic
    D. dynamic

Explanation: To convert a basic disk to a dynamic disk by using DiskPart, open a command prompt, and then type diskpart. At the DISKPART prompt, type list disk. At the DISKPART prompt, type select disk and then enter the number of the disk you are converting. At the DISKPART prompt, type convert dynamic.

29. (QID 29) Which of the following commands would compress the IIS directory?

    A. compact c:\windows\IIS\. /c

    B. compact c:\IIS\..

    C. compact /c c:\Windows

    D. compact /c c:\Windows\.

    E. compact /c c:\IIS\.

---

30. (QID 30) In which of the following scenarios does a file or folder inherit target attributes?

    A. If you copy a compressed file or folder within an NTFS partition to an uncompressed folder

    B. If you move a compressed file or folder within an NTFS partition to an uncompressed folder

    C. When you copy a file to a folder that already contains a file of the same name, the copied file takes on the compression attribute of the target file, regardless of the compression state of the folder.

    D. Files that are moved or copied from a folder on a FAT volume to a folder on an NTFS volume inherit the compression attribute of the target folder.

29. (QID 29) Which of the following commands would compress the IIS directory?

    A. compact c:\windows\IIS\. /c
    B. compact c:\IIS\..
    C. compact /c c:\Windows
    D. compact /c c:\Windows\.
***E. compact /c c:\IIS\.**

Explanation: When used without parameters, compact displays the compression state of the current directory and any files that it contains. For example, you can use the following command line to compress all files and folders in the IIS directory: compact /c c:\IIS\..

30. (QID 30) In which of the following scenarios does a file or folder inherit target attributes?

***A. If you copy a compressed file or folder within an NTFS partition to an uncompressed folder**

    B. If you move a compressed file or folder within an NTFS partition to an uncompressed folder

***C. When you copy a file to a folder that already contains a file of the same name, the copied file takes on the compression attribute of the target file, regardless of the compression state of the folder.**

***D. Files that are moved or copied from a folder on a FAT volume to a folder on an NTFS volume inherit the compression attribute of the target folder.**

Explanation: If you copy a compressed file or folder within an NTFS partition to an uncompressed folder, the file or folder is automatically uncompressed. If you move a compressed file or folder within an NTFS partition to an uncompressed folder, the file remains compressed. When you copy a file or folder between NTFS partitions, the file or folder inherits the compression state of the target folder. When you move a file or folder between NTFS partitions, the file or folder inherits the compression state of the target folder. When you copy a file to a folder that already contains a file of the same name, the copied file takes on the compression attribute of the target file, regardless of the compression state of the folder. Files that are moved or copied from a folder on a FAT volume to a folder on an NTFS volume inherit the compression attribute of the target folder.

31. (QID 31) How can you perform real-time monitoring by using Task Manager?

    A. Press CTRL+ALT+DEL, and then click Task Manager.

    B. Press ALT+SHFT+ESC, and then click Task Manager.

    C. Press CTRL+ALT+ESC, and then click Task Manager.

    D. On the Processes tab, click a column name to sort by that column. Click the column name a second time to reverse sort by that column. On the View menu, click Select Columns to add counters to the Processes tab.

    E. Click the Applications tab to monitor running applications. Click the Processes tab to monitor the running processes.

---

32. (QID 32) You need to install two expansion cards in your 2003 Server. One of the cards is a PCI Plug and Play compliant card and one is an ISA Plug and Play compliant card. What actions are necessary to configure these cards?

    A. With the PCI card, simply plug in the device.

    B. With the ISA card, simply plug in the device.

    C. With the PCI card, you will have to manually configure the card.

    D. With the ISA card, turn off the computer to install the device, and then restart the computer to initialize the device.

    E. With the ISA card, you will have to manually configure the card.

31. (QID 31) How can you perform real-time monitoring by using Task Manager?

***A. Press CTRL+ALT+DEL, and then click Task Manager.**

   B. Press ALT+SHFT+ESC, and then click Task Manager.

   C. Press CTRL+ALT+ESC, and then click Task Manager.

***D. On the Processes tab, click a column name to sort by that column. Click the column name a second time to reverse sort by that column. On the View menu, click Select Columns to add counters to the Processes tab.**

***E. Click the Applications tab to monitor running applications. Click the Processes tab to monitor the running processes.**

Explanation: To perform real-time monitoring by using Task Manager, press CTRL+ALT+DEL, and then click Task Manager. Click the Applications tab to monitor running applications. Click the Processes tab to monitor the running processes. On the Processes tab, click a column name to sort by that column. Click the column name a second time to reverse sort by that column. On the View menu, click Select Columns to add counters to the Processes tab. Click the Performance tab to monitor CPU and memory usage. Click the Networking tab to monitor network traffic to this computer. Click the Users tab to monitor the names of users who are connected to the computer.

---

32. (QID 32) You need to install two expansion cards in your 2003 Server. One of the cards is a PCI Plug and Play compliant card and one is an ISA Plug and Play compliant card. What actions are necessary to configure these cards?

***A. With the PCI card, simply plug in the device.**

   B. With the ISA card, simply plug in the device.

   C. With the PCI card, you will have to manually configure the card.

***D. With the ISA card, turn off the computer to install the device, and then restart the computer to initialize the device.**

   E. With the ISA card, you will have to manually configure the card.

Explanation: You can install some Plug and Play devices by simply plugging in the device. For other devices, such as Plug and Play Industry Standard Architecture (ISA) cards, you must turn off the computer to install the device, and then restart the computer to initialize the device. Most devices manufactured since 1995 are Plug and Play. Plug and Play support depends on both the hardware device and the device driver. If the device driver does not support Plug and Play, its devices behave as non-Plug and Play devices, regardless of any hardware Plug and Play support. Non-Plug and Play devices are not supported by products in the Windows Server 2003 family.

33. (QID 33) Which of the following are options regarding unsigned driver response in Windows 2003?

    A. Quarantining device drivers that are not digitally signed

    B. Saving device drivers that are not digitally signed

    C. Preventing users from installing device drivers that are not digitally signed.

    D. Ignoring device drivers that are not digitally signed

    E. Displaying a warning when Windows detects device drivers that are not digitally signed

34. (QID 34) You tell your junior administrator that you want him to convert all the basic disks in the 2003 Server to dynamic disks. He asks you why this is beneficial. Which of the following would be appropriate responses?

    A. You can create up to 8 volumes per dynamic disk.

    B. With dynamic disks, you can create volumes that span multiple disks.

    C. With dynamic disks, you don't have to defrag as often.

    D. Beyond available drive letters, there isn't a limit on the number of volumes per disk that you can configure.

    E. Dynamic disks can be used to create fault-tolerant disks, ensuring data integrity when hard drive failures take place.

33. (QID 33) Which of the following are options regarding unsigned driver response in Windows 2003?

   A. Quarantining device drivers that are not digitally signed
   B. Saving device drivers that are not digitally signed
***C. Preventing users from installing device drivers that are not digitally signed.**
***D. Ignoring device drivers that are not digitally signed**
***E. Displaying a warning when Windows detects device drivers that are not digitally signed**

Explanation: An administrator can configure Windows to respond to an unsigned device in one of three ways: ignore device drivers that are not digitally signed, display a warning when it detects device drivers that are not digitally signed, or prevent users from installing device drivers that are not digitally signed.

---

34. (QID 34) You tell your junior administrator that you want him to convert all the basic disks in the 2003 Server to dynamic disks. He asks you why this is beneficial. Which of the following would be appropriate responses?

   A. You can create up to 8 volumes per dynamic disk.
***B. With dynamic disks, you can create volumes that span multiple disks.**
   C. With dynamic disks, you don't have to defrag as often.
***D. Beyond available drive letters, there isn't a limit on the number of volumes per disk that you can configure.**
***E. Dynamic disks can be used to create fault-tolerant disks, ensuring data integrity when hard drive failures take place.**

Explanation: With dynamic disks, you can create volumes that span multiple disks. Beyond available drive letters, there isn't a limit on the number of volumes per disk that you can configure. Dynamic disks can be used to create fault-tolerant disks, ensuring data integrity when hard drive failures take place.

35. (QID 35) Viewing hardware devices either by Resources by type or Resources by connection allows you to view devices in which of the following manner?

    A. By manufacturer

    B. By IRQ levels

    C. By I/O and memory addresses

    D. By port number

    E. By DMA (Direct Memory Access) channels

---

36. (QID 36) You want to create a spanned volume from free space from Disk O and Disk 1. Disk 0 has 20 percent of its drive space free and Disk 1 has the entire disk free. Disk 0 is a basic disk and Disk 1 is a dynamic disk and both are formatted with NTFS. What steps do you need to take to create the spanned volume?

    A. Convert Disk 1 back to a basic disk

    B. Convert Disk 0 to a dynamic disk

    C. Create the spanned volume using both dynamic disks

    D. Create the spanned volume using both basic disks

35. (QID 35) Viewing hardware devices either by Resources by type or Resources by connection allows you to view devices in which of the following manner?

    A. By manufacturer
***B. By IRQ levels**
***C. By I/O and memory addresses**
    D. By port number
***E. By DMA (Direct Memory Access) channels**

Explanation: Viewing hardware devices either by Resources by type or Resources by connection allows you to view devices by DMA (Direct Memory Access) channels, IRQ levels, I/O and memory addresses.

---

36. (QID 36) You want to create a spanned volume from free space from Disk O and Disk 1. Disk 0 has 20 percent of its drive space free and Disk 1 has the entire disk free. Disk 0 is a basic disk and Disk 1 is a dynamic disk and both are formatted with NTFS. What steps do you need to take to create the spanned volume?

    A. Convert Disk 1 back to a basic disk
***B. Convert Disk 0 to a dynamic disk**
***C. Create the spanned volume using both dynamic disks**
    D. Create the spanned volume using both basic disks

Explanation: To create a spanned volume, convert Disk 0 to a dynamic disk so that both disks are dynamic. Then simply right-click the unallocated space and select 'New Volume'.

37. (QID 37) You want to create a striped volume from free space from Disk O and Disk 1. Disk 0 has 30 percent of its drive space free and Disk 1 has the entire disk free. Disk 0 is a basic disk and Disk 1 is a dynamic disk and both are formatted with NTFS. What steps do you need to take to create the striped volume?

    A. Convert Disk 0 to a dynamic disk

    B. Convert Disk 1 back to a basic disk

    C. Create the striped volume using both dynamic disks

    D. Create the striped volume using both basic disks

---

38. (QID 38) You want to create a mirrored volume from free space located on Disk O and Disk 1. Disk 0 has 30 percent of its drive space free and Disk 1 has the entire disk free. Disk 0 is a basic disk and Disk 1 is a dynamic disk and both are formatted with NTFS. What steps do you need to take to create the mirrored volume?

    A. Convert Disk 1 back to a basic disk

    B. Convert Disk 0 to a dynamic disk

    C. Create the mirrored volume using both basic disks

    D. Create the mirrored volume using both dynamic disks

37. (QID 37) You want to create a striped volume from free space from Disk O and Disk 1. Disk 0 has 30 percent of its drive space free and Disk 1 has the entire disk free. Disk 0 is a basic disk and Disk 1 is a dynamic disk and both are formatted with NTFS. What steps do you need to take to create the striped volume?

***A. Convert Disk 0 to a dynamic disk**

B. Convert Disk 1 back to a basic disk

***C. Create the striped volume using both dynamic disks**

D. Create the striped volume using both basic disks

Explanation: To create a striped volume, convert Disk 0 to a dynamic disk so that both disks are dynamic. Then simply right-click the unallocated space and select 'New Volume'.

---

38. (QID 38) You want to create a mirrored volume from free space located on Disk O and Disk 1. Disk 0 has 30 percent of its drive space free and Disk 1 has the entire disk free. Disk 0 is a basic disk and Disk 1 is a dynamic disk and both are formatted with NTFS. What steps do you need to take to create the mirrored volume?

A. Convert Disk 1 back to a basic disk

***B. Convert Disk 0 to a dynamic disk**

C. Create the mirrored volume using both basic disks

***D. Create the mirrored volume using both dynamic disks**

Explanation: To create a mirrored volume, convert Disk 0 to a dynamic disk so that both disks are dynamic. Then simply right-click the unallocated space and select 'New Volume'.

39. (QID 39) You want to create a RAID-5 volume from free space from Disk O, Disk 1 and Disk 2. Disk 0 has 30 percent of its drive space free and Disks 1 and 2 have the entire disk free. Disk 0 is a basic disk and Disks 1 and 2 are dynamic disks and all are formatted with NTFS. What steps do you need to take to create the RAID-5 volume?

A. Convert Disk 0 to a dynamic disk

B. Convert Disk 1 back to a basic disk

C. Create the RAID-5 volume using all basic disks

D. Create the RAID-5 volume using all dynamic disks

40. (QID 40) Under what circumstances would you need to update a driver in Windows 2003 server?

A. If you need to convert to NTFS

B. If you need to convert to native mode

C. A bad driver was installed

D. If you have driver signing set to ignore driver updates.

39. (QID 39) You want to create a RAID-5 volume from free space from Disk O, Disk 1 and Disk 2. Disk 0 has 30 percent of its drive space free and Disks 1 and 2 have the entire disk free. Disk 0 is a basic disk and Disks 1 and 2 are dynamic disks and all are formatted with NTFS. What steps do you need to take to create the RAID-5 volume?

***A. Convert Disk 0 to a dynamic disk**

    B. Convert Disk 1 back to a basic disk

    C. Create the RAID-5 volume using all basic disks

***D. Create the RAID-5 volume using all dynamic disks**

Explanation: To create a RAID-5 volume, convert Disk 0 to a dynamic disk so that all disks are dynamic. Then simply right-click the unallocated space and select 'New Volume'.

---

40. (QID 40) Under what circumstances would you need to update a driver in Windows 2003 server?

    A. If you need to convert to NTFS

    B. If you need to convert to native mode

***C. A bad driver was installed**

***D. If you have driver signing set to ignore driver updates.**

Explanation: You need to update a driver in Windows 2003 server if you have driver signing set to ignore driver updates or if a bad driver was installed.

41. (QID 41) What actions would you need to take if you notice a yellow exclamation mark next to a device in Device Manager?

A. Disable the device

B. Update its driver

C. Rollback the driver

D. Reinstall its driver

42. (QID 42) If you want to control device driver installation in regards to digital signatures, which of the following should you use?

A. Task Manager

B. Driver signing

C. Device Manager

D. Event Monitor

41. (QID 41) What actions would you need to take if you notice a yellow exclamation mark next to a device in Device Manager?

>   A. Disable the device
> ***B. Update its driver**
>   C. Rollback the driver
> ***D. Reinstall its driver**

Explanation: If you notice a yellow exclamation mark next to a device in Device Manager, you will need to update or reinstall the device driver to get the hardware to work properly.

---

42. (QID 42) If you want to control device driver installation in regards to digital signatures, which of the following should you use?

>   A. Task Manager
> ***B. Driver signing**
>   C. Device Manager
>   D. Event Monitor

Explanation: If you want to control device driver installation in regards to digital signatures, use Driver signing.

43. (QID 43) Which of the following can Device Manager help you with?

    A. Installation of device drivers

    B. Building device drivers

    C. Rollback device drivers

    D. Updating device drivers

    E. Editing device drivers

---

44. (QID 44) Which of the following utilities will allow you to digitally sign device drivers?

    A. CODE.EXE

    B. SIGNCD.EXE

    C. SIGNCODE.EXE

    D. SIGNDD.EXE

43. (QID 43) Which of the following can Device Manager help you with?

***A. Installation of device drivers**
>   B. Building device drivers

***C. Rollback device drivers**

***D. Updating device drivers**
>   E. Editing device drivers

Explanation: Device Manager can help you with installing, un-installing, rollback, and updating device drivers.

---

44. (QID 44) Which of the following utilities will allow you to digitally sign device drivers?

>   A. CODE.EXE

>   B. SIGNCD.EXE

***C. SIGNCODE.EXE**

>   D. SIGNDD.EXE

Explanation: The SIGNCODE utility will allow you to digitally sign device drivers.

45. (QID 45) How would you go about giving a higher priority to a hardware device?

   A. Make a RAM Drive

   B. Assign it a higher IRQ number than the one it has

   C. Place it in virtual memory

   D. Assign it a lower IRQ number than the one it has

---

46. (QID 46) Which of the following disks can Windows 2003 support?

   A. Basic

   B. Dynamic

   C. Hyper

   D. Cross-pollenated

45. (QID 45) How would you go about giving a higher priority to a hardware device?

    A. Make a RAM Drive
    B. Assign it a higher IRQ number than the one it has
    C. Place it in virtual memory
***D. Assign it a lower IRQ number than the one it has**

Explanation: Assign a device a lower IRQ number than the one it has to give it a higher priority than it had before.

---

46. (QID 46) Which of the following disks can Windows 2003 support?

***A. Basic**
***B. Dynamic**
    C. Hyper
    D. Cross-pollenated

Explanation: Windows 2000/2003 supports both basic and dynamic disks. Basic disks use partitions and dynamic disks use volumes. A Basic disk supports up to four primary partitions or three primary partitions and an extended volume, which can contain logical drives, each with their own assigned drive letter. A dynamic drive isn't limited in the amount of volumes it can have (save drive letters). Dynamic disks are only accessible by Windows 2000, XP, and 2003 machines.

47. (QID 47) Which of the following can a basic disk support in Windows 2003?

    A. Three extended volumes and a primary partition

    B. Four primary partitions

    C. Three primary partitions and an extended volume

    D. Four extended volumes

48. (QID 48) Which of the following machines can access a dynamic volume?

    A. Windows 98, NT, 2000 and 2003 machines

    B. Windows 2000, XP, and 2003 machines

    C. Windows 98, NT, and 2000 machines

    D. Windows 98, NT, XP, and 2003 machines

47. (QID 47) Which of the following can a basic disk support in Windows 2003?

    A. Three extended volumes and a primary partition

***B. Four primary partitions**

***C. Three primary partitions and an extended volume**

    D. Four extended volumes

Explanation: Windows 2000/2003 supports both basic and dynamic disks. Basic disks use partitions and dynamic disks use volumes. A Basic disk supports up to four primary partitions or three primary partitions and an extended volume, which can contain logical drives, each with their own assigned drive letter. A dynamic drive isn't limited in the amount of volumes it can have (save drive letters). Dynamic disks are only accessible by Windows 2000, XP, and 2003 machines.

---

48. (QID 48) Which of the following machines can access a dynamic volume?

***A. Windows 98, NT, 2000 and 2003 machines**

    B. Windows 2000, XP, and 2003 machines

    C. Windows 98, NT, and 2000 machines

    D. Windows 98, NT, XP, and 2003 machines

Explanation: Windows 2000/2003 supports both basic and dynamic disks. Basic disks use partitions and dynamic disks use volumes. A Basic disk supports up to four primary partitions or three primary partitions and an extended volume, which can contain logical drives, each with their own assigned drive letter. A dynamic drive isn't limited in the amount of volumes it can have (save drive letters). Dynamic disks are only accessible by Windows 2000, XP, and 2003 machines.

49. (QID 49) Which of the following should you use to check device drivers, to see if they are installed correctly?

A. My Computer

B. Event Monitor

C. Task Manager

D. Device Manager

E. Internet Options

---

50. (QID 50) You have three SCSI drives. The first drive is a 80 GB drive with 10 GB free. The second drive is a 60 GB drive with 20 GB free. The third drive is a 50 GB drive with the entirety of the drive free. You want to build a RAID-5 array. How big will it be?

A. 10 GB

B. 40 GB

C. 20 GB

D. 80 GB

E. 60 GB

49. (QID 49) Which of the following should you use to check device drivers, to see if they are installed correctly?

***A. My Computer**
  B. Event Monitor
  C. Task Manager
  D. Device Manager
  E. Internet Options

Explanation: Use Device Manager to check device drivers, to see if they are installed correctly.

---

50. (QID 50) You have three SCSI drives. The first drive is a 80 GB drive with 10 GB free. The second drive is a 60 GB drive with 20 GB free. The third drive is a 50 GB drive with the entirety of the drive free. You want to build a RAID-5 array. How big will it be?

  A. 10 GB
  B. 40 GB
***C. 20 GB**
  D. 80 GB
  E. 60 GB

Explanation: With RAID-5, smallest free portion available determines the parity portion of the array (which in this case is 10 GB on the first disk). Since 10 GB is the biggest parity segment we can have, the other portions must be the same size. So, the RAID-5 array will use 30 GB (10 GB + 10 GB + 10 GB), but, you will only be able to use 20 GB of that.

51. (QID 51) You have three SCSI drives. The first drive is a 50 GB drive with 20 GB free. The second drive is an 80 GB drive with 30 GB free. The third drive is a 90 GB drive with the entirety of the drive free. You want to build a RAID-5 array. How big will it be?

    A. 20 GB

    B. 10 GB

    C. 40 GB

    D. 80 GB

    E. 60 GB

52. (QID 52) If you want to remove a device driver from the computer's memory, what benefits can this provide?

    A. Bad device drivers, once removed, only cause page faults

    B. Once you find a suitable driver, you can install it as the replacement

    C. If a device driver is faulty or causing you grief, it will cease from doing so once the driver is removed

    D. If a device driver is faulty or causing you grief, it will only cause a few problems once the driver is removed

51. (QID 51) You have three SCSI drives. The first drive is a 50 GB drive with 20 GB free. The second drive is an 80 GB drive with 30 GB free. The third drive is a 90 GB drive with the entirety of the drive free. You want to build a RAID-5 array. How big will it be?

> A. 20 GB
> B. 10 GB

***C. 40 GB**

> D. 80 GB
> E. 60 GB

Explanation: With RAID-5, the parity portion of the array is determined by the smallest free portion available (which in this case is 20 GB on first disk). Since 20 GB is the biggest parity segment we can have, the other portions must be the same size. So, the RAID-5 array will use 60 GB (20 GB + 20 GB + 20 GB), but, you will only be able to use 40 GB of that.

---

52. (QID 52) If you want to remove a device driver from the computer's memory, what benefits can this provide?

> A. Bad device drivers, once removed, only cause page faults

***B. Once you find a suitable driver, you can install it as the replacement**
***C. If a device driver is faulty or causing you grief, it will cease from doing so once the driver is removed**

> D. If a device driver is faulty or causing you grief, it will only cause a few problems once the driver is removed

Explanation: If a device driver is faulty or causing you grief, it will cease from doing so once the driver is removed. Once you find a suitable driver, you can install it as the replacement.

53. (QID 53) When would driver rollback be a good and feasible option?

    A. When you install a faulty driver after a good one

    B. When you install a faulty driver for the first time

    C. It will remove a bad driver install from the disk

    D. When no driver updates are available after installing a bad driver after a good driver

54. (QID 54) With driver signing, which option should you select if you don't care what drivers are installed?

    A. Unassign

    B. Ignore

    C. Warn

    D. Block

53. (QID 53) When would driver rollback be a good and feasible option?

***A. When you install a faulty driver after a good one**

    B. When you install a faulty driver for the first time

***C. It will remove a bad driver install from the disk**

***D. When no driver updates are available after installing a bad driver after a good driver**

Explanation: When you install a faulty driver after a good one, it would be a good idea to perform driver rollback. When no driver updates are available after installing a bad driver after a good driver, you should perform driver rollback. It will remove a bad driver install from the disk.

---

54. (QID 54) With driver signing, which option should you select if you don't care what drivers are installed?

    A. Unassign

***B. Ignore**

    C. Warn

    D. Block

Explanation: Driver signing options are as follows: ignore (allows all drivers to be installed), warn (prompts you with a warning), and block (does not allow unsigned drivers to be installed).

55. (QID 55) You have a DVD player in your Windows 2003 server that isn't designed to play DVDs from the region in which you reside. What options do you have if you want to play DVDs in your server?

A. You can contact the manufacturer and find out if it is possible to change the region on the DVD player

B. You can reinstall the driver for the DVD player

C. You can buy a new DVD player

D. You can change the file system used on the DVD player

---

56. (QID 56) Which of the following RAID implementations sacrifices the capacity of a hard disk for parity striping?

A. RAID 3

B. RAID 0

C. RAID 1

D. RAID 2

E. RAID 5

55. (QID 55) You have a DVD player in your Windows 2003 server that isn't designed to play DVDs from the region in which you reside. What options do you have if you want to play DVDs in your server?

***A. You can contact the manufacturer and find out if it is possible to change the region on the DVD player**

    B. You can reinstall the driver for the DVD player

***C. You can buy a new DVD player**

    D. You can change the file system used on the DVD player

Explanation: You can either contact the manufacturer and find out if it is possible to change the region on the DVD player or purchase a new one.

---

56. (QID 56) Which of the following RAID implementations sacrifices the capacity of a hard disk for parity striping?

    A. RAID 3

    B. RAID 0

    C. RAID 1

    D. RAID 2

***E. RAID 5**

Explanation: RAID 5 sacrifices the capacity of a hard disk for parity striping. So, if you have a five-disk set, only four disks are available for storage.

57. (QID 57) When implementing redundancy in a Windows 2003 server, which methods will work?

    A. Implementing disk spanning

    B. Implementing disk striping with parity (RAID 5)

    C. Implementing disk mirroring (RAID 1)

    D. Implementing disk striping (RAID 0)

---

58. (QID 58) You store backup tapes both off-site and on-site. You are presently performing a normal backup every Monday at 5 p.m. and incremental backups every work night of the week at 5 p.m. Three drives in your RAID 5 array fail Wednesday at noon. What should you do to restore the RAID 5 array?

    A. Using the on-site tapes, restore the RAID 5 array with the normal backup from Monday

    B. Using the on-site tapes, restore the RAID 5 array with the normal backup from Monday and the incremental from Tuesday

    C. Using the off-site tapes, restore the RAID 5 array with the normal backup from Monday and the incremental from Tuesday.

    D. Using the off-site tapes, restore the RAID 5 array with the normal backup from Monday

57. (QID 57) When implementing redundancy in a Windows 2003 server, which methods will work?

    A. Implementing disk spanning
***B. Implementing disk striping with parity (RAID 5)**
***C. Implementing disk mirroring (RAID 1)**
    D. Implementing disk striping (RAID 0)

Explanation: Implementing disk mirroring (RAID 1) and disk striping with parity (RAID 5) addresses the need for redundancy and fault tolerance in a Windows 2003 server.

---

58. (QID 58) You store backup tapes both off-site and on-site. You are presently performing a normal backup every Monday at 5 p.m. and incremental backups every work night of the week at 5 p.m. Three drives in your RAID 5 array fail Wednesday at noon. What should you do to restore the RAID 5 array?

    A. Using the on-site tapes, restore the RAID 5 array with the normal backup from Monday
***B. Using the on-site tapes, restore the RAID 5 array with the normal backup from Monday and the incremental from Tuesday**
    C. Using the off-site tapes, restore the RAID 5 array with the normal backup from Monday and the incremental from Tuesday.
    D. Using the off-site tapes, restore the RAID 5 array with the normal backup from Monday

Explanation: You store backup tapes both off-site and on-site. You are presently performing a normal backup every Monday at 5 p.m. and incremental backups every work night of the week at 5 p.m. Three drives in your RAID 5 array fails Wednesday at noon. Using the on-site tapes, restore the RAID 5 array with the normal backup from Monday and the incremental from Tuesday.

59. (QID 59) Which of the following RAID configurations does not allow for a single disk to fail?

A. RAID 0 (Disk Striping)

B. RAID 1 (Disk Mirroring)

C. Disk Spanning

D. RAID 5 (Disk Striping with Parity)

---

60. (QID 60) Which of the following is a volume that Windows 2003 server does not support?

A. Spanned

B. RAID 5

C. Half

D. Mirrored

E. RAID 0

59. (QID 59) Which of the following RAID configurations does not allow for a single disk to fail?

***A. RAID 0 (Disk Striping)**

    B. RAID 1 (Disk Mirroring)

***C. Disk Spanning**

    D. RAID 5 (Disk Striping with Parity)

Explanation: RAID 1 (Disk Mirroring) and RAID 5 (Disk Striping with Parity) allow for a single disk to fail. RAID 0 (Disk Striping), and Disk Spanning does not.

---

60. (QID 60) Which of the following is a volume that Windows 2003 server does not support?

    A. Spanned

    B. RAID 5

***C. Half**

    D. Mirrored

    E. RAID 0

Explanation: Windows 2003 server supports RAID 5, spanned, and mirrored volumes.

61. (QID 61) In Windows 2003, the CONVERT command allows you to convert a FAT or FAT32 partition to NTFS. Which of the following uses the proper syntax to accomplish this on the D: partition?

A. CONVERT C:/FS:NTFS

B. CONVERT D:/FS:FAT

C. CONVERT D:/FS:NTFS

D. CONVERT D:

---

64. (QID 62) If you have a multiple-boot hard drive, which of the following Windows 2003 files can be edited to alter those multiple boot options?

A. WIN.INI

B. MS-DOS.SYS

C. BOOT.INI

D. SYSTEM.INI

61. (QID 61) In Windows 2003, the CONVERT command allows you to convert a FAT or FAT32 partition to NTFS. Which of the following uses the proper syntax to accomplish this on the D: partition?

    A. CONVERT C:/FS:NTFS

    B. CONVERT D:/FS:FAT

***C. CONVERT D:/FS:NTFS**

    D. CONVERT D:

Explanation: The proper syntax to convert the D: partition to NTFS is CONVERT D:/FS:NTFS.

---

64. (QID 62) If you have a multiple-boot hard drive, which of the following Windows 2003 files can be edited to alter those multiple boot options?

    A. WIN.INI

    B. MS-DOS.SYS

***C. BOOT.INI**

    D. SYSTEM.INI

Explanation: If you have a multiple-boot hard drive, the BOOT.INI file can be edited to alter those multiple boot options. This is where the boot options are stored for Windows 2003.

Managing Users, Computers, and Groups

The objective of this chapter is to provide the reader with an understanding of the following:

2.1 Manage user profiles

2.1.1 Local user profiles
2.1.2 Roaming user profiles
2.1.3 Mandatory user profiles

2.2 Create and manage computer accounts in an Active Directory environment

2.3 Create and manage groups

2.3.1 Identify and modify the scope of a group
2.3.2 Find domain groups in which a user is a member
2.3.3 Manage group membership
2.3.4 Create and modify groups by using the Active Directory Users and Computers Microsoft Management Console (MMC) snap-in
2.3.5 Create and modify groups by using automation

2.4 Create and manage user accounts

2.4.1 Create and modify user accounts by using the Active Directory Users and Computers MMC snap-in
2.4.2 Create and modify user accounts by using automation
2.4.3 Import user accounts

2.5 Troubleshoot computer accounts

2.5.1 Diagnose and resolve issues related to computer accounts by using the Active Directory Users and Computers MMC snap-in
2.5.2 Reset computer accounts

2.6 Troubleshoot user accounts

2.6.1 Diagnose and resolve account lockouts
2.6.2 Diagnose and resolve issues related to user account properties

2.7 Troubleshoot user authentication issues

Chapter 2: Users, Computers, & Groups

1. (QID 63) You suspect that a user's profile or their account might be corrupted. What actions can you take to figure out which is the case?

   A. Create a new user account and give it the same rights and group memberships or associations as the account that has the profile that you suspect may be damaged.

   B. Copy the user settings in the suspect profile to the profile of the newly created user account. Click Start, point to Control Panel, and then click the System applet.

   C. Create an administrative account and give it the same rights and group memberships or associations as the account that has the profile that you suspect may be damaged.

   D. Click Advanced, and then under User Profiles, click Settings. Under Profiles stored on this computer, click the suspect user profile, and then click Copy To. In the Copy To dialog box, click Browse. Locate the drive:\Documents and Settings\user_profile folder, where drive is the drive where Windows is installed, and where user_profile is the name of the newly created user profile, and then click OK. Click OK, click Yes to overwrite the folder contents, and then click OK two times. Use the newly-created user account to log on.

1. (QID 63) You suspect that a user's profile or their account might be corrupted. What actions can you take to figure out which is the case?

***A. Create a new user account and give it the same rights and group memberships or associations as the account that has the profile that you suspect may be damaged.**
***B. Copy the user settings in the suspect profile to the profile of the newly created user account. Click Start, point to Control Panel, and then click the System applet.**

> C. Create an administrative account and give it the same rights and group memberships or associations as the account that has the profile that you suspect may be damaged.

***D. Click Advanced, and then under User Profiles, click Settings. Under Profiles stored on this computer, click the suspect user profile, and then click Copy To. In the Copy To dialog box, click Browse. Locate the drive:\Documents and Settings\user_profile folder, where drive is the drive where Windows is installed, and where user_profile is the name of the newly created user profile, and then click OK. Click OK, click Yes to overwrite the folder contents, and then click OK two times. Use the newly-created user account to log on.**

Explanation: If you want to check to see if a user account has a damaged profile, create a new user account. Give it the same rights and group memberships or associations as the account that has the profile that you suspect may be damaged. Copy the user settings in the suspect profile to the profile of the newly created user account. Click Start, point to Control Panel, and then click the System applet. Click Advanced, and then under User Profiles, click Settings. Under Profiles stored on this computer, click the suspect user profile, and then click Copy To.

In the Copy To dialog box, click Browse. Locate the drive:\Documents and Settings\user_profile folder, where drive is the drive where Windows is installed, and where user_profile is the name of the newly created user profile, and then click OK. Click OK, click Yes to overwrite the folder contents, and then click OK two times. Use the newly-created user account to log on. If you experience the same errors that led you to question the suspect user profile, the user profile is damaged. If you do not experience any errors, it is the user account that is damaged.

2. (QID 64) How can you make a roaming profile mandatory?

    A. You have to rename the Ntuser.asc file as Ntuser.moc in the user's profile folder

    B. You have to rename the Ntuser.dat file as Ntuser.man in the user's profile folder

    C. You have to rename the Ntuser.asc file as Ntuser.dat in the user's profile folder

    D. You have to rename the Ntuser.dat file as Ntuser.moc in the user's profile folder

---

3. (QID 75) Which of the following does a remote administrator have control over by using regedit?

    A. The number of persons who can be denied access

    B. How frequently the failed attempts counter is reset

    C. The number of failed attempts before future attempts are denied

    D. The number of persons who can be allowed access

2. (QID 64) How can you make a roaming profile mandatory?

    A. You have to rename the Ntuser.asc file as Ntuser.moc in the user's profile folder

***B. You have to rename the Ntuser.dat file as Ntuser.man in the user's profile folder**

    C. You have to rename the Ntuser.asc file as Ntuser.dat in the user's profile folder

    D. You have to rename the Ntuser.dat file as Ntuser.moc in the user's profile folder

Explanation: To create a roaming profile, click Start, point to Administrative Tools, and then click Computer Management. In the console tree, expand Local Users and Groups, and then click Users. Right-click Users, and then click New User. Type a name and password for the user. Click to clear User must change password at next logon. Click Create, and then click Close. Log on as the test user account that you just created. A user profile is automatically created on the local computer in the drive:\Documents and Settings\username folder (where drive is the drive on which Windows is installed). Configure it as you like and log off. Log back on as Administrator. Create a folder on a network drive in which you can store network profiles (\\server_name\Profiles\user_name). Click Start, point to Control Panel, and then click System.

Click the Advanced tab, and then click Settings in the User Profiles section of the System Properties dialog box. Under Profiles Stored On This Computer, click the profile for the user that you created in the 'Create a Test Profile' section of this article, and then click Copy To. In the Copy Profile To dialog box, type the network path to the folder. Under Permitted to Use, click Change. Type the name of the user account that you created in the 'Create a Test Profile' section, and then click OK. Click OK three times. Click Start, point to Administrative Tools, and then click Computer Management. In the console tree, expand Local Users and Groups, and then double-click Users. Double-click the user account that you created. Click the Profile tab. In the Profile path box, type the path to the network profile folder. Click OK. To make this profile mandatory, rename the Ntuser.dat file as Ntuser.man in the user's profile folder.

---

3. (QID 75) Which of the following does a remote administrator have control over by using regedit?

    A. The number of persons who can be denied access

***B. How frequently the failed attempts counter is reset**

***C. The number of failed attempts before future attempts are denied**

    D. The number of persons who can be allowed access

Explanation: Remote access server administrators can adjust the number of failed attempts before future attempts are denied as well as how frequently the failed attempts counter is reset.

4. (QID 65) You want to create a custom default user profile for anyone who logs on to a Computer called Public01. What actions will set it up to use a customer default user profile?

A. Log on to the computer with administrative rights. Create a new local user account. Log off and log back on to the computer with the local user account that you created. Configure the account. Log off and log back on to the computer as administrator.

B. Log on to the computer with administrative rights. Create a new Administrative account. Log off and log back on to the computer with the local user account that you created. Configure the account. Log off and log back on to the computer as administrator.

C. Start Windows Explorer. On the Tools menu, click Folder Options. Click the View tab. Click Show hidden files and folders, and then click OK.

D. Click Start, point to Control Panel, and then click System. Click the Advanced tab. Under User Profiles, click Settings. In the Profiles stored on this computer list, click the user profile that you created, and then click Copy To. In the Copy profile to box, click Browse, click the drive:\Documents and Settings\Default User folder, where drive is the drive on which Windows is installed, and then click OK. Under Permitted to use, click Change. Type Everyone in the Select User or Group box, click OK, and then click OK. Click Yes when you are prompted whether you want to continue to operation. Click OK, and then click OK.

4. (QID 65) You want to create a custom default user profile for anyone who logs on to a Computer called Public01. What actions will set it up to use a customer default user profile?

***A. Log on to the computer with administrative rights. Create a new local user account. Log off and log back on to the computer with the local user account that you created. Configure the account. Log off and log back on to the computer as administrator.**

B. Log on to the computer with administrative rights. Create a new Administrative account. Log off and log back on to the computer with the local user account that you created. Configure the account. Log off and log back on to the computer as administrator.

***C. Start Windows Explorer. On the Tools menu, click Folder Options. Click the View tab. Click Show hidden files and folders, and then click OK.**

***D. Click Start, point to Control Panel, and then click System. Click the Advanced tab. Under User Profiles, click Settings. In the Profiles stored on this computer list, click the user profile that you created, and then click Copy To. In the Copy profile to box, click Browse, click the drive:\Documents and Settings\Default User folder, where drive is the drive on which Windows is installed, and then click OK. Under Permitted to use, click Change. Type Everyone in the Select User or Group box, click OK, and then click OK. Click Yes when you are prompted whether you want to continue to operation. Click OK, and then click OK.**

Explanation: To create a custom default user profile, log on to the computer with administrative rights. Create a new local user account. Log off and log back on to the computer with the local user account that you created. Configure the account. Log off and log back on to the computer as administrator. Start Windows Explorer. On the Tools menu, click Folder Options. Click the View tab. Click Show hidden files and folders, and then click OK. Click Start, point to Control Panel, and then click System. Click the Advanced tab. Under User Profiles, click Settings.

In the Profiles stored on this computer list, click the user profile that you created, and then click Copy To. In the Copy profile to box, click Browse, click the drive:\Documents and Settings\Default User folder, where drive is the drive on which Windows is installed, and then click OK. Under Permitted to use, click Change. Type Everyone in the Select User or Group box, click OK, and then click OK. Click Yes when you are prompted whether you want to continue to operation. Click OK, and then click OK.

5. (QID 66) How can you configure a computer account so that it can be trusted for delegation in Windows Server 2003?

   A. In Active Directory Users and Computers, click Computers. Right-click the computer that you want to configure, and then click Properties. Click the Advanced tab, click Trust this computer for delegation to any service (Kerberos only) , and then click OK.

   B. In Active Directory Domains and Trusts, click Computers. Right-click the computer that you want to configure, and then click Properties. Click the General tab, click Trust this computer for delegation to any service (Kerberos only) , and then click OK.

   C. In Active Directory Sites and Services, click Computers. Right-click the computer that you want to configure, and then click Properties. Click the Delegation tab, click Trust this computer for delegation to any service (Kerberos only) , and then click OK.

   D. In Active Directory Users and Computers, click Computers. Right-click the computer that you want to configure, and then click Properties. Click the Delegation tab, click Trust this computer for delegation to any service (Kerberos only) , and then click OK.

---

6. (QID 67) How can you configure a user account so that it can be trusted for delegation in Windows Server 2003?

   A. Double-click the user that you want to configure

   B. Right-click the user that you want to configure, and then click Properties.

   C. Click the Delegation tab, click Trust this user for delegation to any service (Kerberos only) , and then click OK.

   D. In Active Directory Sites and Services, click Users.

   E. In Active Directory Users and Computers, click Users.

5. (QID 66) How can you configure a computer account so that it can be trusted for delegation in Windows Server 2003?

    A. In Active Directory Users and Computers, click Computers. Right-click the computer that you want to configure, and then click Properties. Click the Advanced tab, click Trust this computer for delegation to any service (Kerberos only) , and then click OK.

    B. In Active Directory Domains and Trusts, click Computers. Right-click the computer that you want to configure, and then click Properties. Click the General tab, click Trust this computer for delegation to any service (Kerberos only) , and then click OK.

    C. In Active Directory Sites and Services, click Computers. Right-click the computer that you want to configure, and then click Properties. Click the Delegation tab, click Trust this computer for delegation to any service (Kerberos only) , and then click OK.

***D. In Active Directory Users and Computers, click Computers. Right-click the computer that you want to configure, and then click Properties. Click the Delegation tab, click Trust this computer for delegation to any service (Kerberos only) , and then click OK.**

Explanation: If you want to configure a computer account so that it can be trusted for delegation in Windows Server 2003, click Start, click Control Panel, double-click Administrative Tools, and then double-click Active Directory Users and Computers. In the console tree, click Computers. Right-click the computer that you want to configure, and then click Properties. Click the Delegation tab, click Trust this computer for delegation to any service (Kerberos only) , and then click OK.

---

6. (QID 67) How can you configure a user account so that it can be trusted for delegation in Windows Server 2003?

    A. Double-click the user that you want to configure

***B. Right-click the user that you want to configure, and then click Properties.**

***C. Click the Delegation tab, click Trust this user for delegation to any service (Kerberos only) , and then click OK.**

    D. In Active Directory Sites and Services, click Users.

***E. In Active Directory Users and Computers, click Users.**

Explanation: If you want to configure a user account so that it can be trusted for delegation in Windows Server 2003, click Start, click Control Panel, double-click Administrative Tools, and then double-click Active Directory Users and Computers. In the console tree, click Users. Right-click the user that you want to configure, and then click Properties. Click the Delegation tab, click Trust this user for delegation to any service (Kerberos only) , and then click OK.

7. (QID 68) Which of the following options gives you the ability to log on even with a disabled local Administrator account on a 2003 Server?

   A. Run the Defragment Tool

   B. Use Recovery Console

   C. Start Windows 2003 in Safe Mode

   D. Boot from a network card that is PXE compliant

---

8. (QID 78) Group scoping is based on which of the following?

   A. The number of users in the group

   B. The security filtering on the GPO.

   C. The WMI filter on the GPO.

   D. The site, domain, or organization unit where the GPO is linked.

7. (QID 68) Which of the following options gives you the ability to log on even with a disabled local Administrator account on a 2003 Server?

  A. Run the Defragment Tool
***B. Use Recovery Console**
***C. Start Windows 2003 in Safe Mode**
  D. Boot from a network card that is PXE compliant

Explanation: To log on to Windows 2003 by using the disabled local Administrator account, start Windows in Safe mode. Even when the Administrator account is disabled, you are not prevented from logging on as Administrator in Safe mode. When you have logged on successfully in Safe mode, re-enable the Administrator account, and then log on again. Start the computer, and then press the F8 key when the Power On Self Test (POST) is complete. From the Windows Advanced Options menu, select Safe Mode. Log on to Windows as Administrator.

If you are prompted to do so, click to select an item in the Why did the computer shut down unexpectedly list, and then click OK. On the message that states Windows is running in safe mode, click OK. Click Start, right-click My Computer, and then click Manage. Expand Local Users and Groups, click Users, right-click Administrator in the right pane, and then click Properties. Click to clear the Account is disabled check box, and then click OK. You can also use the recovery console to access the computer even if the local Administrator account is disabled. Disabling the local Administrator account does not prevent you from logging on to the recovery console as Administrator.

---

8. (QID 78) Group scoping is based on which of the following?

  A. The number of users in the group
***B. The security filtering on the GPO.**
***C. The WMI filter on the GPO.**
***D. The site, domain, or organization unit where the GPO is linked.**

Explanation: Scoping a GPO is based on the site(s), domain(s), or organization unit(s) where the GPO is linked, the security filtering on the GPO, and the WMI filter on the GPO.

9. (QID 69) You Windows 2003 Server has a disabled local Administrator account. After starting up in Safe Mode, what steps can you take to reactivate that Administrative account?

A. Click Start, right-click My Computer, and then click Explore.

B. Expand Local Users and Groups, click Users, right-click Administrator in the right pane, and then click Properties.

C. Click to clear the Account is disabled check box, and then click OK.

D. Click Start, right-click My Computer, and then click Manage.

E. Expand Local Users and Groups, click Users, right-click Guest in the right pane, and then click Properties.

10. (QID 79) How can you backup group policy objects in Server 2003?

A. You can use GPO backup scripts.

B. On the Group Policy Objects node, you can right click and choose the Back Up Default Policies.

C. With GPMC, you can right click one or more GPOs in the Contents tab of the Group Policy objects node and choose Back up from the context menu.

D. With GPMC, Right click a GPO under the Group Policy objects node and choose Back up from the context menu.

9. (QID 69) You Windows 2003 Server has a disabled local Administrator account. After starting up in Safe Mode, what steps can you take to reactivate that Administrative account?

   A. Click Start, right-click My Computer, and then click Explore.

***B. Expand Local Users and Groups, click Users, right-click Administrator in the right pane, and then click Properties.**

***C. Click to clear the Account is disabled check box, and then click OK.**

***D. Click Start, right-click My Computer, and then click Manage.**

   E. Expand Local Users and Groups, click Users, right-click Guest in the right pane, and then click Properties.

Explanation: To log on to Windows 2003 by using the disabled local Administrator account, start Windows in Safe mode. Even when the Administrator account is disabled, you are not prevented from logging on as Administrator in Safe mode. When you have logged on successfully in Safe mode, re-enable the Administrator account, and then log on again. Start the computer, and then press the F8 key when the Power On Self Test (POST) is complete. From the Windows Advanced Options menu, select Safe Mode. Log on to Windows as Administrator.

If you are prompted to do so, click to select an item in the Why did the computer shut down unexpectedly list, and then click OK. On the message that states Windows is running in safe mode, click OK. Click Start, right-click My Computer, and then click Manage. Expand Local Users and Groups, click Users, right-click Administrator in the right pane, and then click Properties. Click to clear the Account is disabled check box, and then click OK. You can also use the recovery console to access the computer even if the local Administrator account is disabled. Disabling the local Administrator account does not prevent you from logging on to the recovery console as Administrator.

10. (QID 79) How can you backup group policy objects in Server 2003?

***A. You can use GPO backup scripts.**

   B. On the Group Policy Objects node, you can right click and choose the Back Up Default Policies.

***C. With GPMC, you can right click one or more GPOs in the Contents tab of the Group Policy objects node and choose Back up from the context menu.**

***D. With GPMC, Right click a GPO under the Group Policy objects node and choose Back up from the context menu.**

Explanation: To backup group policy objects with GPMC, right click a GPO under the Group Policy objects node and choose Back up from the context menu. You can also right click one or more GPOs in the Contents tab of the Group Policy objects node and choose Back up from the context menu. This will backup the selected GPO(s). On the Group Policy Objects node, you can right click and choose the Back Up All option. Finally, you can use GPO backup scripts. Sample scripts are included with GPMC in the GPMC\scripts folder titled BackupGPO.wsf and BackupAllGPOs.wsf.

11. (QID 70) You have just finished editing the default domain policy for your domain, but you do not want this policy to apply to Administrators. What should you do to prevent this?

A. Delete the user or group from the policy.

B. Add the user or group if you need to.

C. Click the administrators group (or other group or user) that you do not want the policy to apply to. In the Permissions windows, click to select the Deny check box for the Apply Group Policy permission.

D. Open Active Directory Users and Computers and right-click the name of the domain where the policy is applied, and then click Properties. Click the Group Policy tab and select the default domain policy. Click Properties, and then click the Security tab.

E. Open Active Directory Domains and Trusts and right-click the name of the domain where the policy is applied, and then click Properties. Click the Group Policy tab and select the default domain policy. Click Properties, and then click the Security tab.

---

12. (QID 81) Which of the following password options is not used in a secure environment?

A. User must change password at the next logon

B. Password never expires

C. User cannot change password

D. Account is disabled

11. (QID 70) You have just finished editing the default domain policy for your domain, but you do not want this policy to apply to Administrators. What should you do to prevent this?

    A. Delete the user or group from the policy.

***B. Add the user or group if you need to.**

***C. Click the administrators group (or other group or user) that you do not want the policy to apply to. In the Permissions windows, click to select the Deny check box for the Apply Group Policy permission.**

***D. Open Active Directory Users and Computers and right-click the name of the domain where the policy is applied, and then click Properties. Click the Group Policy tab and select the default domain policy. Click Properties, and then click the Security tab.**

    E. Open Active Directory Domains and Trusts and right-click the name of the domain where the policy is applied, and then click Properties. Click the Group Policy tab and select the default domain policy. Click Properties, and then click the Security tab.

Explanation: If you want to prevent group policies from applying to Administrator accounts, click Start, point to Administrative Tools, and then click Active Directory Users and Computers. In the left console tree, right-click the name of the domain where the policy is applied, and then click Properties. Click the Group Policy tab. Click the group policy object that you do not want to apply to administrators. By default, the only policy that is listed in the window is the Default Domain Policy. Click Properties, and then click the Security tab. If the group or user who you do not want policies to apply does not appear in the list, Click Add. Click the domain where the account resides.

Find the account, and then click it in the list. Click Add, and then click OK. Click the administrators group (or other group or user) to which you do not want the policy to apply. In the Permissions window, click to select the Deny check box for the Apply Group Policy permission. This prevents the group policy object from being accessed and applied to the selected group or user account.

12. (QID 81) Which of the following password options is not used in a secure environment?

    A. User must change password at the next logon

***B. Password never expires**

    C. User cannot change password

    D. Account is disabled

Explanation: Password options when creating a user account are as follows: User must change password at the next logon, user cannot change password, password never expires (a bad security idea), and Account is disabled.

13. (QID 72) Which of the following is the proper way to format the netdom command if you are attempting to reset the password on a Windows 2003 domain controller named svr12 in a domain called tiger?

A. netdom resetpswd /s:srv12 /ud:domain\User /pd:

B. netdom resetpwd /s:srv12 /ud:tiger\User /pd:

C. netdom resetpwd /s:Servertwelve /ud:tgr\User /pd:

D. netdom resetpwd /s:server /ud:tiger\User /pd:

13. (QID 72) Which of the following is the proper way to format the netdom command if you are attempting to reset the password on a Windows 2003 domain controller named svr12 in a domain called tiger?

    A. netdom resetpswd /s:srv12 /ud:domain\User /pd:

***B. netdom resetpwd /s:srv12 /ud:tiger\User /pd:**

    C. netdom resetpwd /s:Servertwelve /ud:tgr\User /pd:

    D. netdom resetpwd /s:server /ud:tiger\User /pd:

Explanation: You can use Netdom.exe to reset a machine account password. You will need to install the Support Tools for Windows Server 2003 on the domain controller whose password you want to reset. These tools are located in the Tools folder in the Support folder on the Windows Server 2003 CD-ROM. To install these tools, right-click the Suptools.msi file in the Support\Tools folder, and then click Install. If you want to reset the password for a Windows domain controller, you must stop the Kerberos Key Distribution Center service and set its startup type to Manual. After you restart and verify that the password has been successfully reset, you can restart the Kerberos Key Distribution Center service and set its startup type back to Automatic.

This forces the domain controller with the incorrect computer account password to contact another domain controller for a Kerberos ticket. Click Start, Run, and type cmd and click OK. Now type the following command: netdom resetpwd /s:server /ud:domain\User /pd: The /s:server is the name of the domain controller to use for setting the machine account password. The /ud:domain\User is the user account that makes the connection with the domain you specified in the /s parameter. This must be in domain\User format. If this parameter is omitted, the current user account is used. The /pd: specifies the password of the user account that is specified in the /ud parameter. Use an asterisk () to be prompted for the password.

For example, the local domain controller computer is Server1 and the peer Windows domain controller is Server2. If you run Netdom.exe on Server1 with the following parameters, the password is changed locally and is simultaneously written on Server2, and replication propagates the change to other domain controllers: netdom resetpwd /s:server2 /ud:mydomain\administrator /pd: Restart the server whose password was changed. In this example, this is Server1.

14. (QID 71) What should you do if you want to install support tools on a 2003 domain controller?

A. Right-click the Suptools.msi file in the Support\Tools folder, and then click Install.

B. Right-click the Suptools.mst file in the Support\Tools folder, and then click Open.

C. Right-click the Suptools.msc file in the Support\Tools folder, and then click Run.

D. Right-click the Suptools.asc file in the Tools folder, and then click Run.

14. (QID 71) What should you do if you want to install support tools on a 2003 domain controller?

***A. Right-click the Suptools.msi file in the Support\Tools folder, and then click Install.**

   B. Right-click the Suptools.mst file in the Support\Tools folder, and then click Open.

   C. Right-click the Suptools.msc file in the Support\Tools folder, and then click Run.

   D. Right-click the Suptools.asc file in the Tools folder, and then click Run.

Explanation: You can use Netdom.exe to reset a machine account password. You will need to install the Support Tools for Windows Server 2003 on the domain controller whose password you want to reset. These tools are located in the Tools folder in the Support folder on the Windows Server 2003 CD-ROM. To install these tools, right-click the Suptools.msi file in the Support\Tools folder, and then click Install. If you want to reset the password for a Windows domain controller, you must stop the Kerberos Key Distribution Center service and set its startup type to Manual. After you restart and verify that the password has been successfully reset, you can restart the Kerberos Key Distribution Center service and set its startup type back to Automatic. This forces the domain controller with the incorrect computer account password to contact another domain controller for a Kerberos ticket. Click Start, Run, and type cmd and click OK.

Now type the following command: netdom resetpwd /s:server /ud:domain\User /pd: The /s:server is the name of the domain controller to use for setting the machine account password. The /ud:domain\User is the user account that makes the connection with the domain you specified in the /s parameter. This must be in domain\User format. If this parameter is omitted, the current user account is used. The /pd: specifies the password of the user account that is specified in the /ud parameter. Use an asterisk () to be prompted for the password. For example, the local domain controller computer is Server1 and the peer Windows domain controller is Server2. If you run Netdom.exe on Server1 with the following parameters, the password is changed locally and is simultaneously written on Server2, and replication propagates the change to other domain controllers: netdom resetpwd /s:server2 /ud:mydomain\administrator /pd: Restart the server whose password was changed. In this example, this is Server1.

15. (QID 73) You want to adjust the group scope for a group called Marketing in a domain named Techresources.com. How can this be done?

A. In Active Directory Sites and Services, expand Techresources.com. Click the folder that contains the Marketing group. In the right pane, right-click the Marketing group, and then click Properties. Click the General tab, under Group scope, click the group scope that you want, and then click OK.

B. In Active Directory Domain and Trusts, expand Techresources.com. Click the folder that contains the Marketing group. In the right pane, right-click the Marketing group, and then click Properties. Click the General tab, under Group scope, click the group scope that you want, and then click OK.

C. In Active Directory Users and Computers, expand Techresources.com. Click the folder that contains the Marketing group. In the right pane, right-click the Marketing group, and then click Properties. Click the General tab, under Group scope, click the group scope that you want, and then click OK.

D. In Active Directory Users and Computers, expand Techresources.com. Click the folder that contains the Marketing group. In the right pane, right-click the Marketing group, and then click Properties. Click the Advanced tab, under Group scope, click the group scope that you want, and then click OK.

---

16. (QID 80) Which of the following names is associated with a domain user account in Windows 2003?

A. A pre-Windows 2000 user logon name

B. A user principal logon name

C. An Administrative name

D. A Lightweight Directory Access Protocol relative distinguished name

15. (QID 73) You want to adjust the group scope for a group called Marketing in a domain named Techresources.com. How can this be done?

A. In Active Directory Sites and Services, expand Techresources.com. Click the folder that contains the Marketing group. In the right pane, right-click the Marketing group, and then click Properties. Click the General tab, under Group scope, click the group scope that you want, and then click OK.

B. In Active Directory Domain and Trusts, expand Techresources.com. Click the folder that contains the Marketing group. In the right pane, right-click the Marketing group, and then click Properties. Click the General tab, under Group scope, click the group scope that you want, and then click OK.

***C. In Active Directory Users and Computers, expand Techresources.com. Click the folder that contains the Marketing group. In the right pane, right-click the Marketing group, and then click Properties. Click the General tab, under Group scope, click the group scope that you want, and then click OK.**

D. In Active Directory Users and Computers, expand Techresources.com. Click the folder that contains the Marketing group. In the right pane, right-click the Marketing group, and then click Properties. Click the Advanced tab, under Group scope, click the group scope that you want, and then click OK.

Explanation: To change group scope, click Start, point to All Programs, point to Administrative Tools, and then click Active Directory Users and Computers. In the console tree, expand DomainName, where DomainName is the name of your domain. Click the folder that contains the group. In the right pane, right-click the group, and then click Properties. Click the General tab, under Group scope, click the group scope that you want, and then click OK.

16. (QID 80) Which of the following names is associated with a domain user account in Windows 2003?

***A. A pre-Windows 2000 user logon name**
***B. A user principal logon name**
C. An Administrative name
***D. A Lightweight Directory Access Protocol relative distinguished name**

Explanation: There are four types of names associated with domain user accounts. In Active Directory, each user account consists of a user logon name, a pre-Windows 2000 user logon name (Security Accounts Manager account name), a user principal logon name, and a Lightweight Directory Access Protocol(LDAP) relative distinguished name.

17. (QID 74) You want to reset the account lockout policy for remote access clients to three attempts. How would you go about this?

A. Double-click the MaxDenials value. The default value is zero, which indicates that account lockout is turned off. Leave the number of failed attempts before you want the account to be locked out set to default. Click OK.

B. Double-click the MaxDenials value. The default value is zero, which indicates that account lockout is turned off. Set the number of failed attempts before you want the account to be locked out to three. Click OK.

C. Click Start, click Run, type regedit in the Open box, and then press ENTER. Locate and then click the following registry key: HKEY_USERS\SYSTEM\CurrentControlSet\Services\RemoteAccess\Parameters\AccountLockout.

D. Click Start, click Run, type regedit in the Open box, and then press ENTER. Locate and then click the following registry key: HKEY_LOCAL_MACHINE\SYSTEM\CurrentControlSet\Services\RemoteAccess\Parameters\AccountLockout.

17. (QID 74) You want to reset the account lockout policy for remote access clients to three attempts. How would you go about this?

> A. Double-click the MaxDenials value. The default value is zero, which indicates that account lockout is turned off. Leave the number of failed attempts before you want the account to be locked out set to default. Click OK.

***B. Double-click the MaxDenials value. The default value is zero, which indicates that account lockout is turned off. Set the number of failed attempts before you want the account to be locked out to three. Click OK.**

> C. Click Start, click Run, type regedit in the Open box, and then press ENTER. Locate and then click the following registry key:
> HKEY_USERS\SYSTEM\CurrentControlSet\Services\RemoteAccess\Parameters\ AccountLockout.

***D. Click Start, click Run, type regedit in the Open box, and then press ENTER. Locate and then click the following registry key: HKEY_LOCAL_MACHINE\SYSTEM\CurrentControlSet\Services\RemoteAccess\ Parameters\AccountLockout.**

Explanation: Click Start, click Run, type regedit in the Open box, and then press ENTER. Locate and then click the following registry key: HKEY_LOCAL_MACHINE\SYSTEM\CurrentControlSet\Services\RemoteAccess\ Parameters\AccountLockout. Double-click the MaxDenials value. The default value is zero, which indicates that account lockout is turned off. Type the number of failed attempts before you want the account to be locked out. Click OK. Double-click the ResetTime (mins) value. The default value is 0xb40 which is hexadecimal for 2,880 minutes (two days). Modify this value to meet your network security requirements. Click OK. Quit Registry Editor.

18. (QID 76) What are some of the requirements for installing Microsoft Group Policy Management Console?

    A. Either Windows Server 2003 or Windows XP Professional.

    B. The QFE Q326469 hotfix, which updates your version of gpedit.dll to 5.1.2600.1186.

    C. Windows Advanced Server 2003 and Windows XP Home with Service Pack 1 (SP1) and the Microsoft .NET Framework.

    D. Either Windows Server 2003 or Windows XP Professional with Service Pack 1 (SP1) and the Microsoft .NET Framework.

19. (QID 83) Using the dsadd command, which of the following would create an account in the domain domain.com for John Smith with a password of password?

    A. dsadd user 'cn=jsmith,cn=users' -samid user -upn jsmith -fn john -ln smith -display 'user' -pwd password.

    B. dsadd user 'dc=domain,dc=com' -samid user -upn domain.com -fn john -ln smith -display 'user' -pwd password.

    C. dsadd user 'cn=jsmith,cn=users,dc=domain,dc=com' -samid user -upn jsmith@domain.com -fn john -ln smith -display 'user' -pwd password.

    D. dsadd user 'cn=jsmith,cn=users,dc=domain,dc=com' -samid user -upn jsmith@domain.com -fn john -ln smith -display 'user' -pwd.

18. (QID 76) What are some of the requirements for installing Microsoft Group Policy Management Console?

    A. Either Windows Server 2003 or Windows XP Professional.

***B. The QFE Q326469 hotfix, which updates your version of gpedit.dll to 5.1.2600.1186.**

    C. Windows Advanced Server 2003 and Windows XP Home with Service Pack 1 (SP1) and the Microsoft .NET Framework.

***D. Either Windows Server 2003 or Windows XP Professional with Service Pack 1 (SP1) and the Microsoft .NET Framework.**

Explanation: Microsoft Group Policy Management Console (GPMC) is a new tool in 2003 Server for Group Policy management. It provides a user interface for ease of use, backups/restores GPOs, imports/exports GPOs and Windows Management Instrumentation filters. it simplifies management of Group Policy security. The requirements to install GPMC aren't that demanding. You need either Windows Server 2003 or Windows XP Professional with Service Pack 1 (SP1) and the Microsoft .NET Framework. You also need the QFE Q326469 hotfix, which updates your version of gpedit.dll to 5.1.2600.1186. This QFE is included with GPMC, and GPMC setup will prompt you to install it.

---

19. (QID 83) Using the dsadd command, which of the following would create an account in the domain domain.com for John Smith with a password of password?

    A. dsadd user 'cn=jsmith,cn=users' -samid user -upn jsmith -fn john -ln smith -display 'user' -pwd password.

    B. dsadd user 'dc=domain,dc=com' -samid user -upn domain.com -fn john -ln smith -display 'user' -pwd password.

***C. dsadd user 'cn=jsmith,cn=users,dc=domain,dc=com' -samid user -upn jsmith@domain.com -fn john -ln smith -display 'user' -pwd password.**

    D. dsadd user 'cn=jsmith,cn=users,dc=domain,dc=com' -samid user -upn jsmith@domain.com -fn john -ln smith -display 'user' -pwd.

Explanation: To create a user account by using dsadd user, from a command prompt, type dsadd user UserDomainName [-samid SAMName] [-upn UPN] [-fn FirstName] [-ln LastName] [-display DisplayName] [-pwd {Passwordl}] Use ' ' if there is a space in any variable. For example, dsadd user 'cn=jsmith,cn=users,dc=domain,dc=com' -samid user -upn jsmith@domain.com -fn john -ln smith -display 'user' -pwd password.

20. (QID 77) You want to install GPMC (Group Policy Management Console). How would you go about this?

    A. In the \Program Files\GPMC folder, double-click the gpmc.msi package, and click Next.

    B. In the \Program Files folder, double-click the gpmc.mst package, and click Next.

    C. Accept the End User License Agreement (EULA), and click Next. Click Close to complete the installation.

    D. In the \Program Files\GP\GPMC folder, double-click the gpmc.zip package, and click Next.

21. (QID 82) You need to create some local accounts on a domain controller, but, when you go to Computer Management to create some, that option isn't available. What is the cause of this?

    A. The domain controller isn't running in Native mode

    B. The domain controller isn't using NTFS

    C. You cannot create local user accounts on a domain controller.

    D. You aren't logged in as Administrator

20. (QID 77) You want to install GPMC (Group Policy Management Console). How would you go about this?

    A. In the \Program Files\GPMC folder, double-click the gpmc.msi package, and click Next.

    B. In the \Program Files folder, double-click the gpmc.mst package, and click Next.

***C. Accept the End User License Agreement (EULA), and click Next. Click Close to complete the installation.**

    D. In the \Program Files\GP\GPMC folder, double-click the gpmc.zip package, and click Next.

Explanation: To install GPMC, the necessary files are installed to the \Program Files\GPMC folder. Double-click the gpmc.msi package, and click Next. Accept the End User License Agreement (EULA), and click Next. Click Close to complete the installation. Upon completion of the installation, the Group Policy tab that appeared on the Property pages of sites, domains, and organizational units (OUs) in the Active Directory snap-ins is updated to provide a direct link to GPMC. The functionality that previously existed on the original Group Policy tab is no longer available since all functionality for managing Group Policy is available through GPMC.

To open the GPMC snap-in directly, click Start, click Run, type GPMC.msc, and then click OK. Click the Group Policy Management shortcut in the Administrative Tools folder on the Start Menu or in the Control Panel. To create a custom MMC console, click Start, click Run, type MMC, and then click OK. Point to File, click Add/Remove Snap-in, click Add, highlight Group Policy Management, click Add, click Close, and then click OK.To repair or remove GPMC, use Add or Remove Programs in Control Panel. Alternatively, run the gpmc.msi package, select the appropriate option, and click Finish.

---

21. (QID 82) You need to create some local accounts on a domain controller, but, when you go to Computer Management to create some, that option isn't available. What is the cause of this?

    A. The domain controller isn't running in Native mode

    B. The domain controller isn't using NTFS

***C. You cannot create local user accounts on a domain controller.**

    D. You aren't logged in as Administrator

Explanation: You cannot create local user accounts on a domain controller.

22. (QID 84) What steps are necessary in creating a shared mandatory profile to ensure company employees will have the same desktop?

    A. Create a temporary user account, configure it, and change the profile from NTUSER.DAT to NTUSER.MAN

    B. Add the path to the profile in the account

    C. Create a local user template

    D. Create a user template in Active Directory

    E. Create a temporary user account, configure it, and change the profile from NTUSER.DAT to NTUSER.MND

---

23. (QID 85) What can the CSVDE command do?

    A. It can export user accounts from Active Directory

    B. It can import local computer accounts

    C. It can import computer accounts into Active Directory

    D. It can create local computer accounts

22. (QID 84) What steps are necessary in creating a shared mandatory profile to ensure company employees will have the same desktop?

***A. Create a temporary user account, configure it, and change the profile from NTUSER.DAT to NTUSER.MAN**
***B. Add the path to the profile in the account**
    C. Create a local user template
***D. Create a user template in Active Directory**
    E. Create a temporary user account, configure it, and change the profile from NTUSER.DAT to NTUSER.MND

Explanation: First, create a temporary user account, configure it, and change the profile from NTUSER.DAT to NTUSER.MAN. Then create a user template in Active Directory, and add the path to the profile in the account.

---

23. (QID 85) What can the CSVDE command do?

***A. It can export user accounts from Active Directory**
    B. It can import local computer accounts
***C. It can import computer accounts into Active Directory**
    D. It can create local computer accounts

Explanation: The CSVDE command can import and export an object into and from Active Directory.

24. (QID 86) Which of the following is a requirement when importing object with CSVDE?

    A. The objects must be in a comma-delimited .doc file

    B. The objects must be in a comma-delimited binary file

    C. The objects must be in a comma-delimited ASCII text file

    D. The objects must be in a rich text file

---

25. (QID 87) When creating groups, what should you remember about domain local security groups?

    A. You can use a domain local security group to give access to resources in all domains in a forest

    B. You can use a domain local security group to give access to resources in all domains in a tree

    C. They allow you to add members from any domain

    D. You can use a domain local security group to give access to resources in the domain where it was created.

24. (QID 86) Which of the following is a requirement when importing object with CSVDE?

      A. The objects must be in a comma-delimited .doc file
      B. The objects must be in a comma-delimited binary file
***C. The objects must be in a comma-delimited ASCII text file**
      D. The objects must be in a rich text file

Explanation: When importing object with CSVDE, the objects must be in a comma-delimited ASCII text file (Notepad will suffice).

---

25. (QID 87) When creating groups, what should you remember about domain local security groups?

      A. You can use a domain local security group to give access to resources in all domains in a forest
      B. You can use a domain local security group to give access to resources in all domains in a tree
***C. They allow you to add members from any domain**
***D. You can use a domain local security group to give access to resources in the domain where it was created.**

Explanation: Domain local security groups allow you to add members from any domain. You can use a domain local security group to give access to resources in the domain where it was created.

26. (QID 88) Which of the following would be a reason to use a distribution group instead of a security group?

    A. When you want to grant access to resources to those in the domain

    B. When you just want to use email

    C. When you want to grant access to resources to those in the forest

    D. When you want to grant access to resources to those in the tree

---

27. (QID 89) When nesting global groups, where should they be placed to give them rights locally and avoid unnecessary overhead?

    A. In another global group

    B. In a universal group

    C. In a distribution group

    D. In a domain local group

26. (QID 88) Which of the following would be a reason to use a distribution group instead of a security group?

    A. When you want to grant access to resources to those in the domain

***B. When you just want to use email**

    C. When you want to grant access to resources to those in the forest

    D. When you want to grant access to resources to those in the tree

Explanation: Security groups are used for grant access and distribution groups are for email.

---

27. (QID 89) When nesting global groups, where should they be placed to give them rights locally and avoid unnecessary overhead?

    A. In another global group

    B. In a universal group

    C. In a distribution group

***D. In a domain local group**

Explanation: When nesting, place global and universal groups in domain local groups. This allows the global and universal groups to gain the rights that the domain local group possesses. Global groups can only contain user accounts, computer accounts, and global groups from the same domain. Universal groups could work but would increase overhead. Distribution groups cannot be used for security purposes.

28. (QID 90) If you run the command secedit/refreshpolicy user_policy/enforce on a domain controller, what will result?

    A. Password policy changes are enforced immediately for users in the domain

    B. Password policy changes are enforced immediately for computers in the domain

    C. Password policy changes are enforced after five minutes for users in the domain

    D. Password policy changes are enforced after five minutes for computers in the domain

29. (QID 91) Which of the following statements are true about group nesting?

    A. Group nesting isn't used to grant permissions to groups

    B. The domain involved has to be in native mode

    C. The domain involved has to be in mixed mode

    D. Group nesting is the placement of a group into another group

28. (QID 90) If you run the command secedit/refreshpolicy user_policy/enforce on a domain controller, what will result?

***A. Password policy changes are enforced immediately for users in the domain**

    B. Password policy changes are enforced immediately for computers in the domain

    C. Password policy changes are enforced after five minutes for users in the domain

    D. Password policy changes are enforced after five minutes for computers in the domain

Explanation: The command secedit/refreshpolicy user_policy/enforce, when run on a domain controller, will enforce password policy changes immediately for users in the domain. To accomplish the same thing for computers in the domain, run the secedit/refreshpolicy machine_policy/enforce command. Secedit is used to immediately refresh policy; Windows 2000 domain controllers will refresh after five minutes without any extra administrative action.

---

29. (QID 91) Which of the following statements are true about group nesting?

    A. Group nesting isn't used to grant permissions to groups

***B. The domain involved has to be in native mode**

    C. The domain involved has to be in mixed mode

***D. Group nesting is the placement of a group into another group**

Explanation: Group nesting is the placement of a group or groups into another group. Generally, you would do this to grant permissions to the groups nested. For example, a global group would be nested in a domain local group to give the global group the permissions of the domain local group. Native mode has to be set for the domain or domains involved.

30. (QID 92) When nesting global groups, where should they be placed to give them rights locally and avoid unnecessary overhead?

   A. In a distribution group

   B. In another global group

   C. In a universal group

   D. In a domain local group

31. (QID 93) Which of the following statements are true about group nesting?

   A. Group nesting isn't used to grant permissions to groups

   B. The domain involved has be in native mode

   C. The domain involved has be in mixed mode

   D. Group nesting is the placement of a group into another group

30. (QID 92) When nesting global groups, where should they be placed to give them rights locally and avoid unnecessary overhead?

    A. In a distribution group
    B. In another global group
    C. In a universal group
***D. In a domain local group**

Explanation: When nesting, place global and universal groups in domain local groups. This allows the global and universal groups to gain the rights that the domain local group possesses. Global groups can only contain user accounts, computer accounts, and global groups from the same domain. Universal groups could work but would increase overhead. Distribution groups cannot be used for security purposes.

---

31. (QID 93) Which of the following statements are true about group nesting?

    A. Group nesting isn't used to grant permissions to groups
***B. The domain involved has be in native mode**
    C. The domain involved has be in mixed mode
***D. Group nesting is the placement of a group into another group**

Explanation: Group nesting is the placement of a group or groups into another group. Generally, you would do this to grant permissions to the groups nested. For example, a global group would be nested in a domain local group to give the global group the permissions of the domain local group. Native mode has to be set for the domain or domains involved.

32. (QID 94) If you needed to only give a specific group remote access to a number of terminal servers, what would you do?

A. Create a domain and move all the servers into it. Create a GPO and link it to the domain. Configure the GPO to allow the members in the group to log on locally.

B. Create a GPO and move all the servers into it. Create another GPO and link it to the GPO. Configure the GPO to allow the members in the group to log on locally.

C. Create an OU and move all the servers into it. Create a GPO and link it to the domain. Configure the GPO to allow the members in the group to log on locally.

D. Create an OU and move all the servers into it. Create a GPO and link it to the OU. Configure the GPO to allow the members in the group to log on locally.

33. (QID 95) Where are local user profile settings found in Windows 2003?

A. C:\Documents and settings

B. C:\Profiles

C. C:\Local users

D. C:\WINNT

32. (QID 94) If you needed to only give a specific group remote access to a number of
terminal servers, what would you do?

    A. Create a domain and move all the servers into it. Create a GPO and link it to
the domain. Configure the GPO to allow the members in the group to log on
locally.

    B. Create a GPO and move all the servers into it. Create another GPO and link it
to the GPO. Configure the GPO to allow the members in the group to log on
locally.

    C. Create an OU and move all the servers into it. Create a GPO and link it to the
domain. Configure the GPO to allow the members in the group to log on locally.

***D. Create an OU and move all the servers into it. Create a GPO and link it to the
OU. Configure the GPO to allow the members in the group to log on locally.**

Explanation: Creating an OU and moving all the servers into it will keep access
restricted to just those servers. Creating a GPO, linking it to the OU, configuring the
GPO to allow the members in the group to log on locally provides the proper
permissions for them to gain access to the terminal servers.

---

33. (QID 95) Where are local user profile settings found in Windows 2003?

***A. C:\Documents and settings**

    B. C:\Profiles

    C. C:\Local users

    D. C:\WINNT

Explanation: Local user profile settings in Windows 2003 are located in the
C:\Documents and settings directory.

34. (QID 99) How would you configure file and folder security for the Users folder on the G: drive on your Windows 2003 server if you want to completely start from scratch?

A. Right-click the Users folder and click Properties. Select the Security tab. Click Advanced. Click to clear the Allow inheritable permissions from parent to propagate to this object and all child objects. Click Remove. Click OK.

B. Click Add. Add the user or group that you want to give access to the folder. Click the user or group in the Group or user names box, and then click to select the Allow or Deny check box next to the permission that you want to allow or deny.

C. Double-click the Users folder and click Properties. Select the Advanced tab. Click Advanced. Click to clear the Allow inheritable permissions from parent to propagate to this object and all child objects. Click Copy. Click OK.

D. Click Add. Add the user or group that you want to give access to the folder. Click the user or group in the Group or user names box, and then click to select the Allow or Deny check box next to the permission that you want to allow or deny.

E. Right-click the Users folder and click Properties. Select the Security tab. Click Advanced. Click to clear the Allow inheritable permissions from parent to propagate to this object and all child objects. Click Remove. Click OK.

34. (QID 99) How would you configure file and folder security for the Users folder on the G: drive on your Windows 2003 server if you want to completely start from scratch?

***A. Right-click the Users folder and click Properties. Select the Security tab. Click Advanced. Click to clear the Allow inheritable permissions from parent to propagate to this object and all child objects. Click Remove. Click OK.**
***B. Click Add. Add the user or group that you want to give access to the folder. Click the user or group in the Group or user names box, and then click to select the Allow or Deny check box next to the permission that you want to allow or deny.**
  C. Double-click the Users folder and click Properties. Select the Advanced tab. Click Advanced. Click to clear the Allow inheritable permissions from parent to propagate to this object and all child objects. Click Copy. Click OK.
***D. Click Add. Add the user or group that you want to give access to the folder. Click the user or group in the Group or user names box, and then click to select the Allow or Deny check box next to the permission that you want to allow or deny.**
***E. Right-click the Users folder and click Properties. Select the Security tab. Click Advanced. Click to clear the Allow inheritable permissions from parent to propagate to this object and all child objects. Click Remove. Click OK.**

Explanation: To configure folder security, start Windows Explorer. Click the drive that contains the folder that you want to configure. Right-click the folder that you want to configure, and then click Properties. Click the Security tab. Click Advanced. Click to clear the Allow inheritable permissions from parent to propagate to this object and all child objects. Include these with entries explicitly defined here check box. In the Security dialog box that appears, click Remove. The inherited permissions are removed. Click OK. To set permissions for a group or user who is not listed in the Group or user names box, click Add. In the Select Users or Groups dialog box that appears, type the names of the groups or users for whom you want to set permissions. Click OK.

The groups and users you added appear in the Group or user names box. To grant or deny a permission in the Permissions for User or Group box, click the user or group in the Group or user names box, and then click to select the Allow or Deny check box next to the permission that you want to allow or deny.

Managing and Maintaining Access to Resources

The objective of this chapter is to provide the reader with an understanding of the following:

3.1 Configure access to shared folders

    3.1.1 Manage shared folder permissions

3.2 Troubleshoot Terminal Services

    3.2.1 Diagnose and resolve issues related to Terminal Services security
    3.2.2 Diagnose and resolve issues related to client access to Terminal Services

3.3 Configure file system permissions

    3.3.1 Verify effective permissions when granting permissions
    3.3.2 Change ownership of files and folders

3.4 Troubleshoot access to files and shared folders

Chapter 3: Access to Resources

1. (QID 96) You want to ensure that your clients respond to your Terminal Server's requests for security. What steps do you need to take?

    A. Click Start, click Run, type gpedit.msc, and then click OK.

    B. Click Start, click Run, type gpmod.moc, and then click OK.

    C. Expand Security Settings in the left pane, right-click the Client (respond only) policy, and then click Assign.

    D. Expand Security Settings in the left pane, right-click the Server (respond only) policy, and then click Distribute.

2. (QID 97) Which of the following are ways that a shared folder can be accessed in Windows 2003?

    A. By its IP address

    B. By its Universal Naming Convention (UNC)

    C. By a mapped network drive

    D. Through My Network Places

1. (QID 96) You want to ensure that your clients respond to your Terminal Server's requests for security. What steps do you need to take?

***A. Click Start, click Run, type gpedit.msc, and then click OK.**

B. Click Start, click Run, type gpmod.moc, and then click OK.

***C. Expand Security Settings in the left pane, right-click the Client (respond only) policy, and then click Assign.**

D. Expand Security Settings in the left pane, right-click the Server (respond only) policy, and then click Distribute.

Explanation: To ensure that your clients respond to your Terminal Server's requests for security, click Start, click Run, type gpedit.msc, and then click OK. Expand Security Settings in the left pane, right-click the Client (respond only) policy, and then click Assign.

---

2. (QID 97) Which of the following are ways that a shared folder can be accessed in Windows 2003?

A. By its IP address

***B. By its Universal Naming Convention (UNC)**

***C. By a mapped network drive**

***D. Through My Network Places**

Explanation: In Windows 2003, a shared folder can be accessed in My Network Places, by its Universal Naming Convention (UNC), or by a mapped network drive.

3. (QID 98) You want to remove the administrative shares on your Windows 2003 server. How can this be accomplished using the registry?

A. click Start, and then click Run. In the Open box, type regedit, and then click OK.

B. Locate, and then click the following registry key:HKEY_LOCAL_MACHINE\SYSTEM\CurrentControlSet\Services\LanmanSer ver\Parameters\AutoShareServer. On the Edit menu, click Modify. In the Value data box, type 0, and then click OK.

C. Click Start, and then click Run. In the Open box, type cmd, and then click OK. Type the following: net stop server (Press Enter) net start server (Press Enter). Type exit to quit Command Prompt.

D. Locate, and then click the following registry key:HKEY_LOCAL_MACHINE\SYSTEM\CurrentControlSet\Services\LanmanSer ver\Parameters\AutoShareServer. On the Edit menu, click Modify. In the Value data box, type 1, and then click OK.

E. Locate, and then click the following registry key:HKEY_LOCAL_MACHINE\SYSTEM\CurrentControlSet\Services\LanmanSer ver\Parameters\AutoShareServer. On the Edit menu, click Modify. In the Value data box, type 2, and then click OK.

---

4. (QID 100) Earl is a user who needs access to the Project folder on your Windows 2003 server. How can you ensure that Earl will have full control over the Projects folder?

A. Assign Full Control to Earl's account

B. Deny Earl's account the Modify permission

C. Deny Earl's account the Read permission

D. Place Earl in a group with the Full Control permission assigned

3. (QID 98) You want to remove the administrative shares on your Windows 2003 server.
   How can this be accomplished using the registry?

***A. click Start, and then click Run. In the Open box, type regedit, and then click
OK.**
***B. Locate, and then click the following registry
key:HKEY_LOCAL_MACHINE\SYSTEM\CurrentControlSet\Services\LanmanSe
rver\Parameters\AutoShareServer. On the Edit menu, click Modify. In the Value
data box, type 0, and then click OK.**
***C. Click Start, and then click Run. In the Open box, type cmd, and then click OK.
Type the following: net stop server (Press Enter) net start server (Press Enter). Type
exit to quit Command Prompt.**
    D. Locate, and then click the following registry
key:HKEY_LOCAL_MACHINE\SYSTEM\CurrentControlSet\Services\LanmanS
erver\Parameters\AutoShareServer. On the Edit menu, click Modify. In the Value
data box, type 1, and then click OK.
    E. Locate, and then click the following registry
key:HKEY_LOCAL_MACHINE\SYSTEM\CurrentControlSet\Services\LanmanS
erver\Parameters\AutoShareServer. On the Edit menu, click Modify. In the Value
data box, type 2, and then click OK.

Explanation: To remove administrative shares and prevent them from being
automatically created in Windows, click Start, and then click Run. In the Open box,
type regedit, and then click OK. Locate, and then click the following registry
key:HKEY_LOCAL_MACHINE\SYSTEM\CurrentControlSet\Services\LanmanSer
ver\Parameters\AutoShareServer. When this value is set to 0 (zero), Windows does
not automatically create administrative shares. Note that this does not apply to the
IPC$ share or shares that you create manually. On the Edit menu, click Modify. In
the Value data box, type 0, and then click OK. Quit Registry Editor. Stop and then
start the Server service. Click Start, and then click Run. In the Open box, type cmd,
and then click OK. At the command prompt, type the following lines. Press ENTER
after each line: net stop server (Press Enter) net start server (Press Enter). Type exit
to quit Command Prompt.

---

4. (QID 100) Earl is a user who needs access to the Project folder on your Windows 2003
   server. How can you ensure that Earl will have full control over the Projects folder?

***A. Assign Full Control to Earl's account**
    B. Deny Earl's account the Modify permission
    C. Deny Earl's account the Read permission
***D. Place Earl in a group with the Full Control permission assigned**
Explanation: You should always avoid using explicit Deny permissions unless there is
no other way to obtain the specific level of permissions that you need. Assign the
permissions you want to give to the user or the group.

5. (QID 101) Users are able to do more in the Backup folder when they log onto the Windows 2003 member server you have made available to users. What might be the problem?

   A. Inherited permissions that are incorrect for the shared resource

   B. The member server doesn't have an NTFS partition

   C. Group memberships that may grant different levels of permissions

   D. The users are in the Everyone group

---

6. (QID 102) Edward has permissions assigned to his account specifically, as well as permissions assigned to groups of which he is a member on the Accounts folder. Some of these permissions are shared permissions and some are NTFS permissions. What permissions will apply to Edward when he connects to the Accounts folder?

   A. His user permissions

   B. His user permissions, group permissions in which he is a member, NTFS permissions, and shared folder permissions

   C. His user permissions and group permissions in which he is a member

   D. His user permissions, group permissions in which he is a member, and NTFS permissions

5. (QID 101) Users are able to do more in the Backup folder when they log onto the Windows 2003 member server you have made available to users. What might be the problem?

***A. Inherited permissions that are incorrect for the shared resource**
    B. The member server doesn't have an NTFS partition
***C. Group memberships that may grant different levels of permissions**
    D. The users are in the Everyone group

Explanation: By default, permissions are inherited from the folder that contains the object. If users have permissions that they shouldn't have when they log on locally, look for both inherited permissions that are incorrect for the shared resource and for group memberships that may grant different levels of permissions.

---

6. (QID 102) Edward has permissions assigned to his account specifically, as well as permissions assigned to groups of which he is a member on the Accounts folder. Some of these permissions are shared permissions and some are NTFS permissions. What permissions will apply to Edward when he connects to the Accounts folder?

    A. His user permissions
***B. His user permissions, group permissions in which he is a member, NTFS permissions, and shared folder permissions**
    C. His user permissions and group permissions in which he is a member
    D. His user permissions, group permissions in which he is a member, and NTFS permissions

Explanation: When you access data over the network, both share permissions and file and folder permissions apply. Share access permissions are combined with any permissions that are assigned directly to the user and those that are assigned to any groups of which the user is a member.

7. (QID 103) You right-click a folder and select the Properties of the folder. However, when you go to change permissions, you find that there isn't a Security tab. Which of the following isn't the problem?

    A. Your hard drive is too small

    B. You are using the FAT file system

    C. You are using the FAT32 file system

    D. You need to run the convert command

---

8. (QID 104) Which of the following are required to use the Run As command?

    A. Access to a Guest account

    B. An Administrative account

    C. Membership in the backup operators group

    D. A user account

7. (QID 103) You right-click a folder and select the Properties of the folder. However, when you go to change permissions, you find that there isn't a Security tab. Which of the following isn't the problem?

***A. Your hard drive is too small**
    B. You are using the FAT file system
    C. You are using the FAT32 file system
    D. You need to run the convert command

Explanation: If you do not have a Security tab in the Properties dialog box of a folder, you are using the FAT or FAT32 file system. Folder permissions are available only on volumes that are formatted with the NTFS file system.

---

8. (QID 104) Which of the following are required to use the Run As command?
    A. Access to a Guest account
***B. An Administrative account**
    C. Membership in the backup operators group
***D. A user account**

Explanation: To use Run as to perform administrative tasks, systems administrators require two user accounts: a user account with basic privileges and an administrative account. Each administrator can have a different administrative account, or all administrators can share one administrative account.

9. (QID 105) How can you use the Run As command?

    A. Right-click a program located on the Start menu, and then click Run as.

    B. Right-click the Taskbar and click Run as.

    C. You can use the Run as command from a command prompt.

    D. You can right-click a program in Windows Explorer, and then click Run as.

---

10. (QID 106) Which of the following is the correct way to use the Run as command in a command-line environment?

    A. runas /user:domain_name program_name

    B. runas program_name

    C. runas /user:domain_name\user_name program_name

    D. runas /user:domain_name\user_name

9. (QID 105) How can you use the Run As command?

***A. Right-click a program located on the Start menu, and then click Run as.**

    B. Right-click the Taskbar and click Run as.

***C. You can use the Run as command from a command prompt.**

***D. You can right-click a program in Windows Explorer, and then click Run as.**

Explanation: To use the Run as command, you can right-click a program located on the Start menu, and then click Run as. You can right-click a program in Windows Explorer, and then click Run as. You can also use the Run as command from a command prompt. This method is typically used for scripting administrative tasks or to start a command shell in the local administrative context. To run Run as from a command prompt, type runas /user:domain_name\user_name program_name

---

10. (QID 106) Which of the following is the correct way to use the Run as command in a command-line environment?

    A. runas /user:domain_name program_name

    B. runas program_name

***C. runas /user:domain_name\user_name program_name**

    D. runas /user:domain_name\user_name

Explanation: To use the Run as command, you can right-click a program located on the Start menu, and then click Run as. You can right-click a program in Windows Explorer, and then click Run as. You can also use the Run as command from a command prompt. This method is typically used for scripting administrative tasks or to start a command shell in the local administrative context. To run Run as from a command prompt, type runas /user:domain_name\user_name program_name

11. (QID 107) You want to setup a shortcut to access Performance using the Run As command. How can you accomplish this?

    A. Right-click the desktop, point to New, and then click Shortcut.

    B. Right-click the taskbar, point to New, and then click Shortcut.

    C. On the Select a Title for the program page, in the Type a name for this shortcut box, type Performance and then click Finish.

    D. On the Create Shortcut page, in the Type the location of the item box, type runas /user:domain\administrator 'mmc %windir%\system32\perfmon.msc' and then click Next.

---

12. (QID 108) You want to set up Software Update Services. What steps do you have to take to accomplish this?

    A. Download Software Update Services from http://www.technet.com/windows2000/windowsupdate/sus/default.asp.

    B. Double-click the SUS101SP1.exe file to begin the installation process and follow the prompts in the wizard.

    C. Download Software Update Services from http://www.microsoft.com/windows2000/windowsupdate/sus/default.asp.

    D. Double-click the SU.exe file to begin the installation process and follow the prompts in the wizard.

11. (QID 107) You want to setup a shortcut to access Performance using the Run As command. How can you accomplish this?

***A. Right-click the desktop, point to New, and then click Shortcut.**

B. Right-click the taskbar, point to New, and then click Shortcut.

***C. On the Select a Title for the program page, in the Type a name for this shortcut box, type Performance and then click Finish.**

***D. On the Create Shortcut page, in the Type the location of the item box, type runas /user:domain\administrator 'mmc %windir%\system32\perfmon.msc' and then click Next.**

Explanation: To set up a Run as shortcut to Performance, right-click the desktop, point to New, and then click Shortcut. On the Create Shortcut page, in the Type the location of the item box, type runas /user:domain\administrator 'mmc%windir%\system32\perfmon.msc' and then click Next. On the Select a Title for the program page, in the Type a name for this shortcut box, type Performance and then click Finish.

---

12. (QID 108) You want to set up Software Update Services. What steps do you have to take to accomplish this?

A. Download Software Update Services from http://www.technet.com/windows2000/windowsupdate/sus/default.asp.

***B. Double-click the SUS101SP1.exe file to begin the installation process and follow the prompts in the wizard.**

***C. Download Software Update Services from http://www.microsoft.com/windows2000/windowsupdate/sus/default.asp.**

D. Double-click the SU.exe file to begin the installation process and follow the prompts in the wizard.

Explanation: If you want to set up Software Update Services on your Windows 2003 Server, download Software Update Services from http://www.microsoft.com/windows2000/windowsupdate/sus/default.asp. Double-click the SUS101SP1.exe file to begin the installation process. In the Setup Wizard, on the Welcome page, click Next. Read and accept the End User License Agreement. Select the Typical check box. Click Install, and then click Finish in the Setup Wizard to open the Software Update Services administration Web site in Internet Explorer.

13. (QID 109) Which of the following actions should you take if, while you are working with Software Updates Services, you receive the 'http 500-12: Application Restarting' error when attempting to browse to the administration Web site?

    A. Reinstall your 2003 Server

    B. Reinstall Software Updates Services

    C. Press F5 to refresh your browser

    D. Press F9 to refresh your browser

---

14. (QID 110) How can you assign user rights in Windows 2003 Server?

    A. Use the MMC console, and add Group Policy Object Editor snap=in.

    B. Use the MMC console, and add User Rights Editor snap-in.

    C. Expand Local Computer Policy, expand Computer Configuration, expand Windows Settings, expand Security Settings, and then expand Local Policies. Click User Rights Assignment. Adjust the rights.

    D. Expand Local Computer Policy, expand Computer Configuration, expand Windows Settings, expand Security Settings, and then expand Audit Policies. Click Computer Rights Assignment. Adjust the rights.

13. (QID 109) Which of the following actions should you take if, while you are working with Software Updates Services, you receive the 'http 500-12: Application Restarting' error when attempting to browse to the administration Web site?

    A. Reinstall your 2003 Server

    B. Reinstall Software Updates Services

***C. Press F5 to refresh your browser**

    D. Press F9 to refresh your browser

Explanation: When using SUS (Software Updates Services), if you try to browse to the administration Web site and you receive the 'http 500-12: Application Restarting' error, press F5 to refresh your browser.

---

14. (QID 110) How can you assign user rights in Windows 2003 Server?

***A. Use the MMC console, and add Group Policy Object Editor snap=in.**

    B. Use the MMC console, and add User Rights Editor snap-in.

***C. Expand Local Computer Policy, expand Computer Configuration, expand Windows Settings, expand Security Settings, and then expand Local Policies. Click User Rights Assignment. Adjust the rights.**

    D. Expand Local Computer Policy, expand Computer Configuration, expand Windows Settings, expand Security Settings, and then expand Audit Policies. Click Computer Rights Assignment. Adjust the rights.

Explanation: To assign user rights, click Start, click Run, type mmc and then press Enter. Click Console. On the File menu, click Add/Remove Snap-in. In the Add/Remove Snap-in dialog box, click Add. In the Add Standalone Snap-in dialog box, double-click Group Policy Object Editor. Click Finish to close the Welcome to Group Policy Wizard. Click Close to close the Add Standalone Snap-in dialog box. Click OK to close the Add/Remove Snap-in dialog box. Expand Local Computer Policy, expand Computer Configuration, expand Windows Settings, expand Security Settings, and then expand Local Policies. Click User Rights Assignment. Add or remove a group to a user right as needed.

15. (QID 111) Which of the following security templates are default security templates?

   A. Setup security.inf

   B. DC security.inf

   C. Compatws.inf

   D. Secure.inf

   E. hisec.inf

---

16. (QID 112) Which of the following security templates is the most secure?

   A. DC security.inf

   B. Compatws.inf

   C. Secure.inf

   D. hisec.inf

15. (QID 111) Which of the following security templates are default security templates?

***A. Setup security.inf**
***B. DC security.inf**
    C. Compatws.inf
    D. Secure.inf
    E. hisec.inf

Explanation: The Setup security.inf template is created during installation of the operating system for each computer and represents default security settings that are applied during installation, including the file permissions for the root of the system drive. The DC security.inf template is created when a server is promoted to a domain controller. It reflects default security settings on files, registry keys, and system services. The Compatws.inf template changes the default file and registry permissions that are granted to the Users group. The Secure templates (Secure.inf) define stronger password, lockout, and audit settings. The Highly Secure templates (hisec.inf) are supersets of the Secure templates and they impose further restrictions on the levels of encryption and signing that are required for authentication and for the data that flows over secure channels and between server message block (SMB) clients and servers. Rootsec.inf defines the permissions for the root of the system drive.

---

16. (QID 112) Which of the following security templates is the most secure?
    A. DC security.inf
    B. Compatws.inf
    C. Secure.inf
***D. hisec.inf**

Explanation: The Setup security.inf template is created during installation of the operating system for each computer and represents default security settings that are applied during installation, including the file permissions for the root of the system drive. The DC security.inf template is created when a server is promoted to a domain controller. It reflects default security settings on files, registry keys, and system services. The Compatws.inf template changes the default file and registry permissions that are granted to the Users group. The Secure templates (Secure.inf) define stronger password, lockout, and audit settings. The Highly Secure templates (hisec.inf) are supersets of the Secure templates and they impose further restrictions on the levels of encryption and signing that are required for authentication and for the data that flows over secure channels and between server message block (SMB) clients and servers. Rootsec.inf defines the permissions for the root of the system drive.

17. (QID 113) You want to import a security template to a local computer named WS01. How can you accomplish this?

    A. In the console tree, right-click Group Policy Editor, and then click Import Template.

    B. In the Import Template dialog box, click a template file, and then click Open.

    C. In the console tree, right-click Security Configuration and Analysis, and then click Import Template.

    D. Open Security Configuration and Analysis.

---

18. (QID 114) You want to enable audit on a folder named Private and you need to know whether or not someone is trying to access the folder, even if they aren't successful. What steps do you need to take?

    A. Right-click the Private folder and select Properties. In the Properties dialog box, on the Security tab, click Advanced. In the Advanced Security Settings dialog box, on the Auditing tab, enable auditing for a new user or group by clicking Add.

    B. Under Access, click only Successful.

    C. In the Enter the object name to select box, type the name of the user or group, and then click OK. If you want to view or change auditing for an existing group or user, click the name, and then click Edit. depending on the type of access that you want to audit.

    D. Under Access, click both Successful and Failed.

17. (QID 113) You want to import a security template to a local computer named WS01. How can you accomplish this?

    A. In the console tree, right-click Group Policy Editor, and then click Import Template.

***B. In the Import Template dialog box, click a template file, and then click Open.**
***C. In the console tree, right-click Security Configuration and Analysis, and then click Import Template.**
***D. Open Security Configuration and Analysis.**

Explanation: To import a security template to a local computer, open Security Configuration and Analysis. In the console tree, right-click Security Configuration and Analysis, and then click Import Template. To clear the database of any template, select the Clear this database before importing check box (this isn't necessary). In the Import Template dialog box, click a template file, and then click Open.

---

18. (QID 114) You want to enable audit on a folder named Private and you need to know whether or not someone is trying to access the folder, even if they aren't successful. What steps do you need to take?

***A. Right-click the Private folder and select Properties. In the Properties dialog box, on the Security tab, click Advanced. In the Advanced Security Settings dialog box, on the Auditing tab, enable auditing for a new user or group by clicking Add.**

    B. Under Access, click only Successful.

***C. In the Enter the object name to select box, type the name of the user or group, and then click OK. If you want to view or change auditing for an existing group or user, click the name, and then click Edit. depending on the type of access that you want to audit.**
***D. Under Access, click both Successful and Failed.**

Explanation: In Windows Explorer, locate the file or folder that you want to audit. Right-click the file or folder, and then click Properties. In the Properties dialog box, on the Security tab, click Advanced. In the Advanced Security Settings dialog box, on the Auditing tab, enable auditing for a new user or group by clicking Add. In the Enter the object name to select box, type the name of the user or group, and then click OK. If you want to view or change auditing for an existing group or user, click the name, and then click Edit. If you want to disable auditing for an existing group or user, click the name, and then click Remove. Under Access, click Successful, Failed, or both Successful and Failed, depending on the type of access that you want to audit. If you want to prevent child objects from inheriting these audit entries, select the Apply these auditing entries to objects and/or containers within this container only check box.

19. (QID 115) You move a group with existing rights and permissions already set from one OU to a new OU. Which of the following statements apply to the group's permissions?

    A. Explicitly set permissions no longer apply.

    B. An object inherits permissions from the organizational unit to which it is moved.

    C. An object no longer inherits permissions from the organizational unit from which it is moved.

    D. Explicitly set permissions remain the same.

20. (QID 116) Which of the following commands will allow you to connect to the console session on a remote server?

    A. The MMC command and the mstsc command line tool.

    B. The Run command and the mstsc command line tool.

    C. The ipconfig command and the mstsc command line tool.

    D. The Run command and the msc command line tool.

19. (QID 115) You move a group with existing rights and permissions already set from one OU to a new OU. Which of the following statements apply to the group's permissions?

    A. Explicitly set permissions no longer apply.
***B. An object inherits permissions from the organizational unit to which it is moved.**
***C. An object no longer inherits permissions from the organizational unit from which it is moved.**
***D. Explicitly set permissions remain the same.**

Explanation: When you move a group into an organization unit, permissions that are set explicitly remain the same. An object inherits permissions from the organizational unit to which it is moved. An object no longer inherits permissions from the organizational unit that from which it is moved.

20. (QID 116) Which of the following commands will allow you to connect to the console session on a remote server?

    A. The MMC command and the mstsc command line tool.
***B. The Run command and the mstsc command line tool.**
    C. The ipconfig command and the mstsc command line tool.
    D. The Run command and the msc command line tool.

Explanation: You can connect to the console session on a remote server by using the Run command and the mstsc command line tool.

21. (QID 117) What is the proper syntax to connect to the console session on a remote server?

    A. mstsc

    B. mstsc /console

    C. mstsc /v:server

    D. mstsc /v:server /console

22. (QID 118) What steps are necessary to configure a timeout setting for a remote connection?

    A. On the Sessions tab, select the last Override user settings check box and adjust the appropriate settings.

    B. On the Sessions tab, select the first Override user settings check box and adjust the appropriate settings.

    C. In the Administrative Tools menu, click Remote Configuration. In the details pane, right-click RDP-Tcp, and then click Properties.

    D. In the Administrative Tools menu, click Terminal Services Configuration. In the details pane, right-click RDP-Tcp, and then click Properties.

21. (QID 117) What is the proper syntax to connect to the console session on a remote server?

    A. mstsc

    B. mstsc /console

    C. mstsc /v:server

***D. mstsc /v:server /console**

Explanation: You can connect to the console session on a remote server by using the Run command and the mstsc command line tool (mstsc /v:server /console).

---

22. (QID 118) What steps are necessary to configure a timeout setting for a remote connection?

    A. On the Sessions tab, select the last Override user settings check box and adjust the appropriate settings.

***B. On the Sessions tab, select the first Override user settings check box and adjust the appropriate settings.**

    C. In the Administrative Tools menu, click Remote Configuration. In the details pane, right-click RDP-Tcp, and then click Properties.

***D. In the Administrative Tools menu, click Terminal Services Configuration. In the details pane, right-click RDP-Tcp, and then click Properties.**

Explanation: To configure a timeout setting for a remote connection, Click Start. On the Administrative Tools menu, click Terminal Services Configuration. In the details pane, right-click RDP-Tcp, and then click Properties. On the Sessions tab, select the first Override user settings check box. Adjust the appropriate settings.

23. (QID 119) Which of the following methods will allow you to install the updated Automatic Updates client on your client computers?

A. Install Windows XP SP1

B. Download the wininst.exe file from the Server 2003 CD-ROM

C. Install Automatic Updates client by using the Windows Installer package(.msi file)

D. Install Windows Server 2003

24. (QID 120) You want to adjust the ability of users in the Administrative group to install unsigned drivers. When they attempt to do this, which of the following options are possible?

A. Silently succeed

B. Warn but allow installation

C. Notify Administrator

D. Do not allow installation

23. (QID 119) Which of the following methods will allow you to install the updated Automatic Updates client on your client computers?

***A. Install Windows XP SP1**
    B. Download the wininst.exe file from the Server 2003 CD-ROM
***C. Install Automatic Updates client by using the Windows Installer package(.msi file)**
***D. Install Windows Server 2003**

Explanation: You can install the updated Automatic Updates client on your client computers by installing Automatic Updates client by using the Windows Installer package(.msi file), installing Windows 2000 Service Pack 3 (SP3), install Windows XP SP1, or installing Windows Server 2003.

---

24. (QID 120) You want to adjust the ability of users in the Administrative group to install unsigned drivers. When they attempt to do this, which of the following options are possible?

***A. Silently succeed**
***B. Warn but allow installation**
    C. Notify Administrator
***D. Do not allow installation**

Explanation: The Unsigned driver installation behavior Group Policy setting has three options: Silently succeed (allows the user to install an unsigned device driver without receiving a warning), Warn but allow installation (allows the user to install an unsigned device driver, but a warning about installing unsigned device drivers is displayed), or Do not allow installation (prevents the installation of unsigned device drivers).

25. (QID 121) You are logged into to a 2003 domain controller with a user account you created. You want to start the Group Policy Manager, but you want to do this with administrative rights. How can you accomplish this without having to log out and log back in with the Administrator account?

    A. Type in the following, runadmin /user:administrator 'mmc %windir%\system32\gpmc.msc'.

    B. Type in the following, run /user:domain\admin 'mmc %windir%\system32\gpmc.msc'.

    C. Type in the following, runas /user:domain\administrator 'mmc %windir%\system32\gpmc.msc'.

    D. Type in the following, runadms /user:domain\administrator 'mmc %windir%\system32\gpmc.msc'.

---

26. (QID 122) If a user contacts you while on call, and tells you that she locked herself out of her account and that she has also forgotten her password, what should you do?

    A. Uncheck the Account is locked out check box in Active Directory for her account

    B. Make her an Administrator

    C. Reset her password

    D. Make her account a local one

25. (QID 121) You are logged into to a 2003 domain controller with a user account you created. You want to start the Group Policy Manager, but you want to do this with administrative rights. How can you accomplish this without having to log out and log back in with the Administrator account?

    A. Type in the following, runadmin /user:administrator 'mmc %windir%\system32\gpmc.msc'.

    B. Type in the following, run /user:domain\admin 'mmc %windir%\system32\gpmc.msc'.

***C. Type in the following, runas /user:domain\administrator 'mmc %windir%\system32\gpmc.msc'.**

    D. Type in the following, runadms /user:domain\administrator 'mmc %windir%\system32\gpmc.msc'.

Explanation: Use runas to start the Group Policy Manager snap-in with administrative privileges: runas /user:domain\administrator 'mmc %windir%\system32\gpmc.msc'.

---

26. (QID 122) If a user contacts you while on call, and tells you that she locked herself out of her account and that she has also forgotten her password, what should you do?

***A. Uncheck the Account is locked out check box in Active Directory for her account**

    B. Make her an Administrator

***C. Reset her password**

    D. Make her account a local one

Explanation: If a user contacts you while on call, and tells you that she locked herself out of her account and that she has also forgotten her password, reset her password and uncheck the Account is locked out check box in Active Directory for her account.

27. (QID 123) What is the difference between Terminal Services remote administration mode and application server mode?

A. Terminal Services remote administration mode requires licensing within 90 days of installation and application server mode requires licensing immediately.

B. Terminal Services remote administration mode requires licensing immediately and application server mode requires licensing within 90 days of installation.

C. Terminal Services remote administration mode does not require any licensing and application server mode requires licensing within 30 days of installation.

D. Terminal Services remote administration mode does not require any licensing and application server mode requires licensing within 90 days of installation.

---

28. (QID 124) If you wanted to limit the time remote access users can access a RRAS server without actually doing anything, which option on the RRAS server should we set?

A. Disconnect if VPN idle for

B. Reconnect if idle for

C. Disconnect if idle for

D. Reconnect if VPN idle for

27. (QID 123) What is the difference between Terminal Services remote administration mode and application server mode?

    A. Terminal Services remote administration mode requires licensing within 90 days of installation and application server mode requires licensing immediately.

    B. Terminal Services remote administration mode requires licensing immediately and application server mode requires licensing within 90 days of installation.

    C. Terminal Services remote administration mode does not require any licensing and application server mode requires licensing within 30 days of installation.

***D. Terminal Services remote administration mode does not require any licensing and application server mode requires licensing within 90 days of installation.**

Explanation: The difference between Terminal Services remote administration mode and application server mode is that Terminal Services remote administration mode does not require any licensing and application server mode requires licensing within 90 days of installation.

---

28. (QID 124) If you wanted to limit the time remote access users can access a RRAS server without actually doing anything, which option on the RRAS server should we set?

    A. Disconnect if VPN idle for

    B. Reconnect if idle for

***C. Disconnect if idle for**

    D. Reconnect if VPN idle for

Explanation: The only option that we can actually set on the RRAS server is the Disconnect if idle for option. This allows dial-up connects that are not being used to be dropped.

29. (QID 125) When shadowing an active session of another user, what can you do?

   A. View but not control the session

   B. View and control the session

   C. Only control the session on the computer where the session was initiated

   D. Only view the session on the computer where the session was initiated

---

30. (QID 126) Slipstreaming a service pack would involve what command?

   A. setup.exe -slpstrm:c:\Win2003

   B. setup.exe -slip:c:\Win2003

   C. setup.exe -s:c:\Win2003

   D. setup.exe -ss:c:\Win2003

29. (QID 125) When shadowing an active session of another user, what can you do?

    A. View but not control the session

***B. View and control the session**

    C. Only control the session on the computer where the session was initiated

    D. Only view the session on the computer where the session was initiated

Explanation: When shadowing an active session of another user, you can either view and control the session from wherever you are by logging into the server running Terminal services. Actively controlling the session with your keyboard and mouse is just like initiating the session.

---

30. (QID 126) Slipstreaming a service pack would involve what command?

    A. setup.exe -slpstrm:c:\Win2003

    B. setup.exe -slip:c:\Win2003

***C. setup.exe -s:c:\Win2003**

    D. setup.exe -ss:c:\Win2003

Explanation: We would use the -s switch with the setup.exe to slipstream a service pack.

31. (QID 127) If you want to give an admin group higher printing priority over the rest of the company's employees when you only have one printing device and no budget for a new printing device, what steps should you take?

A. Create and share an additional printer for the printing device. Set the priority level for that printer to 1. Remove the Everyone group from the second printer. Make sure that the User group has the Allow print permission.

B. Create and share an additional printer for the printing device. Set the priority level for that printer to 99. Remove the Everyone group from the second printer. Make sure that the User group has the Allow print permission.

C. Create and share an additional printer for the printing device. Set the priority level for that printer to 1. Remove the Everyone group from the second printer. Make sure that the Admin group has the Allow print permission.

D. Create and share an additional printer for the printing device. Set the priority level for that printer to 99. Remove the Everyone group from the second printer. Make sure that the Admin group has the Allow print permission.

---

32. (QID 128) The network segment on which your client is located is the 192.168.18 segment. The subnet mask for the network segment is 255.255.255.128 and the router interface for the network segment is 192.168.18.1. The client can't get out of the network segment. The client has an IP address of 192.168.19.5, a subnet mask of 255.255.255.224, and a default gateway of 192.168.17.1. What should you change to allow the client to get out onto the network?

A. Change the IP address to 192.168.18.5. Change the Subnet Mask to 255.255.255.128. Leave the Default Gateway as it is.

B. Change the IP address to 192.168.18.5. Leave the Subnet Mask as it is. Change the Default Gateway to 192.168.18.1.

C. Change the IP address to 192.168.18.5. Change the Subnet Mask to 255.255.255.128. Change the Default Gateway to 192.168.18.1.

D. Leave the IP address as it is. Change the Subnet Mask to 255.255.255.128. Change the Default Gateway to 192.168.18.1.

31. (QID 127) If you want to give an admin group higher printing priority over the rest of the company's employees when you only have one printing device and no budget for a new printing device, what steps should you take?

    A. Create and share an additional printer for the printing device. Set the priority level for that printer to 1. Remove the Everyone group from the second printer. Make sure that the User group has the Allow print permission.

    B. Create and share an additional printer for the printing device. Set the priority level for that printer to 99. Remove the Everyone group from the second printer. Make sure that the User group has the Allow print permission.

    C. Create and share an additional printer for the printing device. Set the priority level for that printer to 1. Remove the Everyone group from the second printer. Make sure that the Admin group has the Allow print permission.

***D. Create and share an additional printer for the printing device. Set the priority level for that printer to 99. Remove the Everyone group from the second printer. Make sure that the Admin group has the Allow print permission.**

Explanation: We can set up an additional printer for the printing device. By setting the priority level for that printer to 99, it will take precedence over the other printer, since 99 is the highest priority and 1 is the lowest. Remove the Everyone group from the second printer (since it is there by default) and make sure that the Admin group has the Allow print permission.

---

32. (QID 128) The network segment on which your client is located is the 192.168.18 segment. The subnet mask for the network segment is 255.255.255.128 and the router interface for the network segment is 192.168.18.1. The client can't get out of the network segment. The client has an IP address of 192.168.19.5, a subnet mask of 255.255.255.224, and a default gateway of 192.168.17.1. What should you change to allow the client to get out onto the network?

    A. Change the IP address to 192.168.18.5. Change the Subnet Mask to 255.255.255.128. Leave the Default Gateway as it is.

    B. Change the IP address to 192.168.18.5. Leave the Subnet Mask as it is. Change the Default Gateway to 192.168.18.1.

***C. Change the IP address to 192.168.18.5. Change the Subnet Mask to 255.255.255.128. Change the Default Gateway to 192.168.18.1.**

    D. Leave the IP address as it is. Change the Subnet Mask to 255.255.255.128. Change the Default Gateway to 192.168.18.1.

Explanation: The network segment on which your client is located is the 192.168.18 segment, not the 192.168.19 segment. The subnet mask for the network segment is 255.255.255.128, not 255.255.255.224 and the router interface for the network segment is 192.168.18.1, not 192.168.17.1.

33. (QID 129) Which of the following might be the cause of network connectivity issues?

A. Insufficient rights (i.e. - the proxy server only allows access to certain persons or sites)

B. Bad IP information (incorrect IP, subnet mask, default gateway)

C. Physical connectivity is down (the server may be down or the cable could have failed)

D. No Answer is Correct

---

34. (QID 130) Which of the following audit events should you enable to monitor misuse of privileges?

A. Success and Failure audit for file-access and object-access events

B. Failure audit for logon/logoff

C. Success audit for logon/logoff

D. Success audit for user rights, user and group management, security change policies, restart, shutdown, and system events

33. (QID 129) Which of the following might be the cause of network connectivity issues?

***A. Insufficient rights (i.e. - the proxy server only allows access to certain persons or sites)**
***B. Bad IP information (incorrect IP, subnet mask, default gateway)**
***C. Physical connectivity is down (the server may be down or the cable could have failed)**
      D. No Answer is Correct

Explanation: If the IP information is wrong or dated (incorrect IP, subnet mask, default gateway), it could stop a client from getting to the Internet. DNS issues (a bad DNS server address, whether it is manually entered or cached) could also be the problem. Insufficient rights or restrictions could the problem, if the client is trying to access the Internet in an improper way. If the issue is physical in nature, which is possible, test the connectivity with ping, tracert, and pathping.

---

34. (QID 130) Which of the following audit events should you enable to monitor misuse of privileges?

      A. Success and Failure audit for file-access and object-access events
      B. Failure audit for logon/logoff
      C. Success audit for logon/logoff
***D. Success audit for user rights, user and group management, security change policies, restart, shutdown, and system events**

Explanation: Use the 'Failure audit for logon/logoff' audit event when you want to monitor random password hacking or brute force attacks. Use the 'Success audit for logon/logoff' audit event when you want to monitor for stolen or unsecured passwords. Use the 'Success audit for user rights, user and group management, security change policies, restart, shutdown, and system events' audit event when you want to monitor misuse of privileges. Use the 'Success and Failure audit for file-access and object-access events' audit event when you want to monitor access to sensitive files.

35. (QID 131) Which of the following audit events should you enable to monitor access to sensitive files?

    A. Success audit for logon/logoff

    B. Failure audit for logon/logoff

    C. Success and Failure audit for file-access and object-access events

    D. Success audit for user rights, user and group management, security change policies, restart, shutdown, and system events

36. (QID 132) When using driver signing options, which of the following options should you choose if you want to prevent installation of unsigned files?

    A. Block

    B. Ignore

    C. Warn

    D. Apply setting as system default

35. (QID 131) Which of the following audit events should you enable to monitor access to sensitive files?

    A. Success audit for logon/logoff

    B. Failure audit for logon/logoff

***C. Success and Failure audit for file-access and object-access events**

    D. Success audit for user rights, user and group management, security change policies, restart, shutdown, and system events

Explanation: Use the 'Failure audit for logon/logoff' audit event when you want to monitor random password hacking or brute force attacks. Use the 'Success audit for logon/logoff' audit event when you want to monitor for stolen or unsecured passwords. Use the 'Success audit for user rights, user and group management, security change policies, restart, shutdown, and system events' audit event when you want to monitor misuse of privileges. Use the 'Success and Failure audit for file-access and object-access events' audit event when you want to monitor access to sensitive files.

---

36. (QID 132) When using driver signing options, which of the following options should you choose if you want to prevent installation of unsigned files?

***A. Block**

    B. Ignore

    C. Warn

***D. Apply setting as system default**

Explanation: When using driver signing options, you have the following options: Ignore, Warn, and Block. Ignore installs all files, regardless of file signature. Warn displays a message before installing an unsigned file. Block prevents installation of unsigned files. There is also an Administrator option: Apply setting as system default, which is necessary to make changes permanent.

37. (QID 133) If you needed to only give a specific group remote access to a number of terminal servers, what would you do?

    A. Create an OU and move all the servers into it. Create a GPO and link it to the domain. Configure the GPO to allow the members in the group to log on locally.

    B. Create a domain and move all the servers into it. Create a GPO and link it to the domain. Configure the GPO to allow the members in the group to log on locally.

    C. Create a GPO and move all the servers into it. Create another GPO and link it to the GPO. Configure the GPO to allow the members in the group to log on locally.

    D. Create an OU and move all the servers into it. Create a GPO and link it to the OU. Configure the GPO to allow the members in the group to log on locally.

---

38. (QID 134) In device manager, what does the yellow icon with an exclamation point in the center signify?

    A. That the device is not OEM.

    B. That the device is not functioning properly.

    C. That the device has been installed in the machine backwards

    D. That the device is brand new

37. (QID 133) If you needed to only give a specific group remote access to a number of terminal servers, what would you do?

    A. Create an OU and move all the servers into it. Create a GPO and link it to the domain. Configure the GPO to allow the members in the group to log on locally.

    B. Create a domain and move all the servers into it. Create a GPO and link it to the domain. Configure the GPO to allow the members in the group to log on locally.

    C. Create a GPO and move all the servers into it. Create another GPO and link it to the GPO. Configure the GPO to allow the members in the group to log on locally.

***D. Create an OU and move all the servers into it. Create a GPO and link it to the OU. Configure the GPO to allow the members in the group to log on locally.**

Explanation: Creating an OU and moving all the servers into it will keep access restricted to just those servers. Creating a GPO, linking it to the OU, configuring the GPO to allow the members in the group to log on locally provides the proper permissions for them to gain access to the terminal servers.

---

38. (QID 134) In device manager, what does the yellow icon with an exclamation point in the center signify?

    A. That the device is not OEM.

***B. That the device is not functioning properly.**

    C. That the device has been installed in the machine backwards

    D. That the device is brand new

Explanation: In device manager, the yellow icon with an exclamation point in the center signifies that the device is not functioning properly.

39. (QID 135) What is the difference between Terminal Services Remote Desktop for Administration mode and application server mode?

    A. Terminal Services remote administration mode requires licensing immediately and application server mode requires licensing within 90 days of installation.

    B. Terminal Services remote administration mode requires licensing within 90 days of installation and application server mode requires licensing immediately.

    C. Terminal Services remote administration mode does not require any licensing and application server mode requires licensing within 90 days of installation.

    D. Terminal Services remote administration mode does not require any licensing and application server mode requires licensing within 30 days of installation.

---

40. (QID 136) How are disk quotas enforced?

    A. Per Domain

    B. Per Volume

    C. Per User

    D. Per Site

39. (QID 135) What is the difference between Terminal Services Remote Desktop for Administration mode and application server mode?

   A. Terminal Services remote administration mode requires licensing immediately and application server mode requires licensing within 90 days of installation.
   B. Terminal Services remote administration mode requires licensing within 90 days of installation and application server mode requires licensing immediately.

***C. Terminal Services remote administration mode does not require any licensing and application server mode requires licensing within 90 days of installation.**

   D. Terminal Services remote administration mode does not require any licensing and application server mode requires licensing within 30 days of installation.

Explanation: The difference between Terminal Services Remote Desktop for Administration and application server mode is that Terminal Services remote administration mode does not require any licensing and application server mode requires licensing within 90 days of installation.

---

40. (QID 136) How are disk quotas enforced?

   A. Per Domain
***B. Per Volume**
***C. Per User**
   D. Per Site

Explanation: Disk quotas are enforced either per volume or per user. So, make sure to keep this in mind when users are working on multiple partitions. It is easier to have all users who need to use disk quotas use the same volume or partition.

41. (QID 137) If you want to give an admin group higher printing priority over the rest of the company's employees when you only have one printing device and no budget for a new printing device, what steps should you take?

    A. Create and share an additional printer for the printing device. Set the priority level for that printer to 99. Remove the Everyone group from the second printer. Make sure that the Admin group has the Allow print permission.

    B. Create and share an additional printer for the printing device. Set the priority level for that printer to 99. Remove the Everyone group from the second printer. Make sure that the User group has the Allow print permission.

    C. Create and share an additional printer for the printing device. Set the priority level for that printer to 1. Remove the Everyone group from the second printer. Make sure that the Admin group has the Allow print permission.

    D. Create and share an additional printer for the printing device. Set the priority level for that printer to 1. Remove the Everyone group from the second printer. Make sure that the User group has the Allow print permission.

---

42. (QID 138) Which of the following disk quota logging options are available to us in Windows 2003?

    A. Log event when a user nears their quota limit

    B. Log event when a user exceeds their quota limit

    C. Log event when a user exceeds their warning level

    D. Log event when a user nears their warning level

41. (QID 137) If you want to give an admin group higher printing priority over the rest of the company's employees when you only have one printing device and no budget for a new printing device, what steps should you take?

***A. Create and share an additional printer for the printing device. Set the priority level for that printer to 99. Remove the Everyone group from the second printer. Make sure that the Admin group has the Allow print permission.**

    B. Create and share an additional printer for the printing device. Set the priority level for that printer to 99. Remove the Everyone group from the second printer. Make sure that the User group has the Allow print permission.

    C. Create and share an additional printer for the printing device. Set the priority level for that printer to 1. Remove the Everyone group from the second printer. Make sure that the Admin group has the Allow print permission.

    D. Create and share an additional printer for the printing device. Set the priority level for that printer to 1. Remove the Everyone group from the second printer. Make sure that the User group has the Allow print permission.

Explanation: We can set up an additional printer for the printing device. By setting the priority level for that printer to 99, it will take precedence over the other printer, since 99 is the highest priority and 1 is the lowest. Remove the Everyone group from the second printer (since it is there by default) and make sure that the Admin group has the Allow print permission.

---

42. (QID 138) Which of the following disk quota logging options are available to us in Windows 2003?

    A. Log event when a user nears their quota limit

***B. Log event when a user exceeds their quota limit**

***C. Log event when a user exceeds their warning level**

    D. Log event when a user nears their warning level

Explanation: In the properties of a volume with the Quota tab selected, we can select the following quota logging options: Log event when a user exceeds their quota limit and Log event when a user exceeds their warning level.

43. (QID 139) Which of the following audit events should you enable to monitor misuse of privileges?

    A. Success and Failure audit for file-access and object-access events

    B. Failure audit for logon/logoff

    C. Success audit for logon/logoff

    D. Success audit for user rights, user and group management, security change policies, restart, shutdown, and system events

---

44. (QID 140) Which of the following audit events should you enable to monitor access to sensitive files?

    A. Success audit for logon/logoff

    B. Failure audit for logon/logoff

    C. Success and Failure audit for file-access and object-access events

    D. Success audit for user rights, user and group management, security change policies, restart, shutdown, and system events

43. (QID 139) Which of the following audit events should you enable to monitor misuse of privileges?

> A. Success and Failure audit for file-access and object-access events
> B. Failure audit for logon/logoff
> C. Success audit for logon/logoff

***D. Success audit for user rights, user and group management, security change policies, restart, shutdown, and system events**

Explanation: Use the 'Failure audit for logon/logoff' audit event when you want to monitor random password hacking or brute force attacks. Use the 'Success audit for logon/logoff' audit event when you want to monitor for stolen or unsecured passwords. Use the 'Success audit for user rights, user and group management, security change policies, restart, shutdown, and system events' audit event when you want to monitor misuse of privileges. Use the 'Success and Failure audit for file-access and object-access events' audit event when you want to monitor access to sensitive files.

---

44. (QID 140) Which of the following audit events should you enable to monitor access to sensitive files?

> A. Success audit for logon/logoff
> B. Failure audit for logon/logoff

***C. Success and Failure audit for file-access and object-access events**

> D. Success audit for user rights, user and group management, security change policies, restart, shutdown, and system events

Explanation: Use the 'Failure audit for logon/logoff' audit event when you want to monitor random password hacking or brute force attacks. Use the 'Success audit for logon/logoff' audit event when you want to monitor for stolen or unsecured passwords. Use the 'Success audit for user rights, user and group management, security change policies, restart, shutdown, and system events' audit event when you want to monitor misuse of privileges. Use the 'Success and Failure audit for file-access and object-access events' audit event when you want to monitor access to sensitive files.

45. (QID 141) How do you get to driver signing in Windows 2003?

A. Right-click My Computer and select properties (System Properties), and choose the Hardware Tab

B. Right-click My Network Places and select properties (System Properties), and choose the Hardware Tab

C. Left-click My Computer and select properties (System Properties), and choose the Hardware Tab

D. Left-click My Network Places and select properties (System Properties), and choose the Hardware Tab

---

46. (QID 142) Which of the following options can be accessed in Computer Management?

A. Event Viewer

B. Domain Users

C. Disk Management

D. Device Manager

E. Domain Groups

45. (QID 141) How do you get to driver signing in Windows 2003?

***A. Right-click My Computer and select properties (System Properties), and choose the Hardware Tab**

   B. Right-click My Network Places and select properties (System Properties), and choose the Hardware Tab

   C. Left-click My Computer and select properties (System Properties), and choose the Hardware Tab

   D. Left-click My Network Places and select properties (System Properties), and choose the Hardware Tab

Explanation: If you want to enable driver signing in Windows 2003, right-click My Computer and select properties (System Properties), and choose the Hardware Tab.

---

46. (QID 142) Which of the following options can be accessed in Computer Management?

***A. Event Viewer**

   B. Domain Users

***C. Disk Management**

***D. Device Manager**

   E. Domain Groups

Explanation: If you want to access Computer Management, right-click the My Computer icon and select the Manage option. Computer Management contains helpful options such as Event Viewer, Device Manager, and Disk Management.

47. (QID 143) How can you access the Device Manager in Windows 2003?

A. Go to Control Panel through the Start Menu, select Classic View, and Select the System icon. From there, select the hardware tab and choose Device Manager.

B. Right-click the My Computer icon and select properties. From there, select the hardware tab and choose Device Manager.

C. Right-click the My Computer icon and select manage. Then choose Device Manager.

D. Right-click the My Network Places icon and select properties. From there, select the hardware tab and choose Device Manager.

---

48. (QID 144) If you want to see what type of NIC card you have installed in your Windows 2003 computer, confirm it in Device Manager. How can you get there?

A. In Control Panel, select the Display option. From there, select the Hardware tab and select Device Manager.

B. Right-click the My Computer icon and select properties. From there, select the Hardware tab and select Device Manager.

C. Right-click the My Computer icon and select manage. This brings up Computer Management that has Device Manager as an option.

D. In Control Panel, select the System option. From there, select the Hardware tab and select Device Manager.

47. (QID 143) How can you access the Device Manager in Windows 2003?

***A. Go to Control Panel through the Start Menu, select Classic View, and Select the System icon. From there, select the hardware tab and choose Device Manager.**
***B. Right-click the My Computer icon and select properties. From there, select the hardware tab and choose Device Manager.**
***C. Right-click the My Computer icon and select manage. Then choose Device Manager.**

      D. Right-click the My Network Places icon and select properties. From there, select the hardware tab and choose Device Manager.

Explanation: If you want to access Device Manager in Windows 2003, there are various ways you can do this. The first way is as follows: go to Control Panel through the Start Menu, select Classic View, and Select the System icon, from there, select the hardware tab and choose Device Manager. Here's the second way: right-click the My Computer icon and select properties, from there, select the hardware tab and choose Device Manager. Here's the third way: right-click the My Computer icon and select manage, then choose Device Manager.

---

48. (QID 144) If you want to see what type of NIC card you have installed in your Windows 2003 computer, confirm it in Device Manager. How can you get there?

      A. In Control Panel, select the Display option. From there, select the Hardware tab and select Device Manager.
***B. Right-click the My Computer icon and select properties. From there, select the Hardware tab and select Device Manager.**
***C. Right-click the My Computer icon and select manage. This brings up Computer Management that has Device Manager as an option.**
***D. In Control Panel, select the System option. From there, select the Hardware tab and select Device Manager.**

Explanation: To access Device Manager, use one of the following methods. In Control Panel, select the System option. From there, select the Hardware tab and select Device Manager. Right-click the My Computer icon and select properties. From there, select the Hardware tab and select Device Manager. Right-click the My Computer icon and select manage. This brings up Computer Management which has Device Manager as an option.

49. (QID 145) Which of the following is not something that Add/Remove Hardware option in Control Panel (Classic View) can do in a Windows 2003 environment?

A. Troubleshoot an existing device

B. Uninstall a device driver

C. Backup the Registry

D. Unplug a device

---

50. (QID 146) A Terminal Services application server can use which of the following operation modes?

A. Edit mode

B. Execute mode

C. Sub mode

D. Hyper mode

E. Install mode

49. (QID 145) Which of the following is not something that Add/Remove Hardware option in Control Panel (Classic View) can do in a Windows 2003 environment?

    A. Troubleshoot an existing device

    B. Uninstall a device driver

***C. Backup the Registry**

    D. Unplug a device

Explanation: The Add/Remove Hardware option in Control Panel in a Windows 2003 environment can uninstall a device driver, troubleshoot an existing device, and unplug a device.

---

50. (QID 146) A Terminal Services application server can use which of the following operation modes?

    A. Edit mode

***B. Execute mode**

    C. Sub mode

    D. Hyper mode

***E. Install mode**

Explanation: A Terminal Services application server has two separate modes of operation: install mode and execute mode. Install mode should be used for installing applications that aren't 'Certified for Windows' (these are generally older programs that don't use Setup.exe or Install.exe).

51. (QID 147) A Terminal Services application server should use which of the following modes for a program not 'Certified for Windows'?

    A. Hyper mode

    B. Execute mode

    C. Install mode

    D. Sub mode

---

52. (QID 148) Which of the following commands allows you to enable or disable logon events to Terminal Services?

    A. Change User

    B. Change logon

    C. Change Port

    D. Change Up

51. (QID 147) A Terminal Services application server should use which of the following modes for a program not 'Certified for Windows'?

    A. Hyper mode

    B. Execute mode

***C. Install mode**

    D. Sub mode

Explanation: A Terminal Services application server has two separate operation modes: install mode and execute mode. Install mode should be used for installing applications that aren't 'Certified for Windows' (these are generally older programs that don't use Setup.exe or Install.exe).

---

52. (QID 148) Which of the following commands allows you to enable or disable logon events to Terminal Services?

    A. Change User

***B. Change logon**

    C. Change Port

    D. Change Up

Explanation: The Change command allows you to change between user modes (install and execute), reassign port mappings for Terminal Services sessions, and enable or disable logon events to Terminal Services.

53. (QID 149) Which of the following describes what can be accomplished with the Change command?

   A. It allows you to change between user modes (install and execute)

   B. It blocks user modes (install and execute)

   C. It can enable or disable logon events to Terminal Services

   D. It can reassign port mappings for Terminal Services sessions

---

54. (QID 150) Which of the following starts the Terminal Services Manager?

   A. Termsadm.exe

   B. Termadmin.exe

   C. Tsadmin.exe

   D. Tservadmin.exe

53. (QID 149) Which of the following describes what can be accomplished with the Change command?

***A. It allows you to change between user modes (install and execute)**

    B. It blocks user modes (install and execute)

***C. It can enable or disable logon events to Terminal Services**

***D. It can reassign port mappings for Terminal Services sessions**

Explanation: The Change command allows you to change between user modes (install and execute), reassign port mappings for Terminal Services sessions, and enable or disable logon events to Terminal Services.

---

54. (QID 150) Which of the following starts the Terminal Services Manager?

    A. Termsadm.exe

    B. Termadmin.exe

***C. Tsadmin.exe**

    D. Tservadmin.exe

Explanation: Tsadmin.exe starts the Terminal Services Manager.

55. (QID 151) Which of the following commands will allow you to send a message to users that have active sessions on a Terminal server?

    A. send

    B. note

    C. alert

    D. post

    E. msg

---

56. (QID 152) Which of the following commands shows the correct syntax to take control of a user's session?

    A. syntax[sessionname|sessionid] [/SERVER:servername] [/V]

    B. control [sessionname|sessionid] [/SERVER:servername] [/V]

    C. take [sessionname|sessionid] [/SERVER:servername] [/V]

    D. grab [sessionname|sessionid] [/SERVER:servername] [/V]

    E. shadow [sessionname|sessionid] [/SERVER:servername] [/V]

55. (QID 151) Which of the following commands will allow you to send a message to users that have active sessions on a Terminal server?

    A. send
    B. note
    C. alert
    D. post
***E. msg**

Explanation: The msg command will allow you to send a message to users that have active sessions on a Terminal server.

---

56. (QID 152) Which of the following commands shows the correct syntax to take control of a user's session?

    A. syntax[sessionname|sessionid] [/SERVER:servername] [/V]
    B. control [sessionname|sessionid] [/SERVER:servername] [/V]
    C. take [sessionname|sessionid] [/SERVER:servername] [/V]
    D. grab [sessionname|sessionid] [/SERVER:servername] [/V]
***E. shadow [sessionname|sessionid] [/SERVER:servername] [/V]**

Explanation: The proper syntax for the shadow command is as follows: shadow [sessionname|sessionid] [/SERVER:servername] [/V]

57. (QID 153) Which of the following directories contains the Remote Desktop Client program?

    A. %windir%\system32\clients\sclient\drivers

    B. %windir%\system32\clients\tsclient

    C. %windir%\system32\clients

    D. %windir%\system32\tsclient\win32

    E. %windir%\system32\clients\tsclient\win32

---

58. (QID 154) Which of the following operating systems can have the Remote Desktop Client program installed on them by using the installation program in the %windir%\system32\clients\tsclient\win32 directory?

    A. Windows NT 4.0, Windows 2000, Windows XP

    B. Windows 95 and 98

    C. Windows XP Home and Professional

    D. Windows XP and Server 2003

    E. All Answers are Correct

57. (QID 153) Which of the following directories contains the Remote Desktop Client program?

    A. %windir%\system32\clients\sclient\drivers
    B. %windir%\system32\clients\tsclient
    C. %windir%\system32\clients
    D. %windir%\system32\tsclient\win32

***E. %windir%\system32\clients\tsclient\win32**

Explanation: The %windir%\system32\clients\tsclient\win32 directory contains the Remote Desktop Client program. This program can be used to install Remote Desktop client on Windows 9x, Me, NT 4.0, 2000, as well as XP and 2003.

---

58. (QID 154) Which of the following operating systems can have the Remote Desktop Client program installed on them by using the installation program in the %windir%\system32\clients\tsclient\win32 directory?

    A. Windows NT 4.0, Windows 2000, Windows XP
    B. Windows 95 and 98
    C. Windows XP Home and Professional
    D. Windows XP and Server 2003

***E. All Answers are Correct**

Explanation: The %windir%\system32\clients\tsclient\win32 directory contains the Remote Desktop Client program. This can install Remote Desktop client on Windows 9x, Me, NT 4.0, 2000, as well as XP and 2003.

59. (QID 155) Which of the following allows you to access the Default Web Site?

    A. Type http://127.0.0.2 in the Run box and click OK

    B. Type http://127.0.0.1 in your browser and hit Enter

    C. Type localhost in the Address bar and press Enter

    D. Type http://127.0.0.1 in the Run box and click OK

60. (QID 156) Which of the following virtual directories are available in Windows 2003?

    A. virtual

    B. Remote

    C. Extended

    D. Expanded

    E. Local

59. (QID 155) Which of the following allows you to access the Default Web Site?

      A. Type http://127.0.0.2 in the Run box and click OK

***B. Type http://127.0.0.1 in your browser and hit Enter**

***C. Type localhost in the Address bar and press Enter**

***D. Type http://127.0.0.1 in the Run box and click OK**

Explanation: To access the Default Web Site, you can type http://127.0.0.1 in either the Run box or in your browser. You can also type localhost in the Address bar and press Enter.

---

60. (QID 156) Which of the following virtual directories are available in Windows 2003?

      A. virtual

***B. Remote**

      C. Extended

      D. Expanded

***E. Local**

Explanation: With local virtual directories, the content is located on the local server. With remote virtual directories, the content is located on a remote file server.

61. (QID 157) Which of the following virtual directories stores content on the IIS server?

    A. virtual

    B. Extended

    C. Expanded

    D. Remote

    E. Local

---

62. (QID 158) Which of the following switches, when used with the iiisreset command, will stop and restart all IIS services?

    A. /start

    B. /restart

    C. /stop

    D. /reboot

61. (QID 157) Which of the following virtual directories stores content on the IIS server?

    A. virtual
    B. Extended
    C. Expanded
    D. Remote

***E. Local**

Explanation: With local virtual directories, the content is located on the local server. With remote virtual directories, the content is located on a remote file server.

---

62. (QID 158) Which of the following switches, when used with the iiisreset command, will stop and restart all IIS services?

    A. /start

***B. /restart**

    C. /stop
    D. /reboot

Explanation: The /restart switch, when used with the iiisreset command, will stop and restart all IIS services.

63. (QID 159) Which of the following switches, when used with the iiisreset command, will start all IIS services?

    A. /reboot

    B. /status

    C. /stop

    D. /start

---

64. (QID 160) Which of the following switches, when used with the iiisreset command, will stop all IIS services?

    A. /start

    B. /status

    C. /stop

    D. /reboot

63. (QID 159) Which of the following switches, when used with the iiisreset command, will start all IIS services?

> A. /reboot
> B. /status
> C. /stop

***D. /start**

Explanation: The /start switch, when used with the iiisreset command, will start all IIS services.

---

64. (QID 160) Which of the following switches, when used with the iiisreset command, will stop all IIS services?

***A. /start**

> B. /status
> C. /stop
> D. /reboot

Explanation: The /stop switch, when used with the iiisreset command, will stop all IIS services.

65. (QID 161) Which of the following switches, when used with the iiisreset command, will reboot the IIS server?

A. /start

B. /status

C. /reboot

D. /restart

---

66. (QID 162) Which of the following HTTP error messages would indicate that the IIS server can't understand the syntax of the request?

A. 400

B. 401

C. 403

D. 404

65. (QID 161) Which of the following switches, when used with the iiisreset command, will reboot the IIS server?

    A. /start
    B. /status
***C. /reboot**
    D. /restart

Explanation: The /reboot switch, when used with the iiisreset command, will reboot the IIS server.

---

66. (QID 162) Which of the following HTTP error messages would indicate that the IIS server can't understand the syntax of the request?

***A. 400**
    B. 401
    C. 403
    D. 404

Explanation: The 400 HTTP error message would indicate that the IIS server can't understand the syntax of the request.

67. (QID 163) Which of the following HTTP error messages would indicate that the user isn't authorized to access the IIS server?

    A. 400

    B. 401

    C. 403

    D. 404

    E. 405

68. (QID 164) Which of the following HTTP error messages would indicate that the user is forbidden access to the IIS server due to a lack of SSL?

    A. 400

    B. 401

    C. 403

    D. 404

    E. 405

67. (QID 163) Which of the following HTTP error messages would indicate that the user isn't authorized to access the IIS server?

    A. 400
*B. 401
    C. 403
    D. 404
    E. 405

Explanation: The 401 HTTP error message would indicate that the user isn't authorized to access the IIS server.

---

68. (QID 164) Which of the following HTTP error messages would indicate that the user is forbidden access to the IIS server due to a lack of SSL?

    A. 400
    B. 401
*C. 403
    D. 404
    E. 405

Explanation: The 403 HTTP error message would indicate that the user is forbidden access to the IIS server due to a lack of SSL.

69. (QID 165) Which of the following HTTP error messages would indicate that the file for which you are looking isn't found?

    A. 400

    B. 401

    C. 402

    D. 404

    E. 405

---

70. (QID 166) Which of the following is the default user account that IIS uses when you specify anonymous access?

    A. IUSR_SERVERNAME

    B. USER_SERVERNAME

    C. IUSR_SERVERNAME

    D. R_SERVERNAME

    E. USR_SERVERNAME

69. (QID 165) Which of the following HTTP error messages would indicate that the file for which you are looking isn't found?

    A. 400
    B. 401
    C. 402
***D. 404**
    E. 405

Explanation: The 404 HTTP error message would indicate that the file for which you are looking isn't found.

---

70. (QID 166) Which of the following is the default user account that IIS uses when you specify anonymous access?

    A. IUSR_SERVERNAME
    B. USER_SERVERNAME
***C. IUSR_SERVERNAME**
    D. R_SERVERNAME
    E. USR_SERVERNAME

Explanation: IUSR_SERVERNAME is the default user account that IIS uses when you specify anonymous access.

71. (QID 167) In an FTP's site properties, what directory listing style is recommended for maximum compatibility?

    A. OS2

    B. MS-DOS

    C. WIN 2000

    D. WIN 2003

    E. UNIX

---

72. (QID 183) You want to create an IPSec filter list for Terminal Services communications. What steps should you take?

    A. Use the TCP port 80

    B. Use the TCP port 3389

    C. Verify that the Mirrored check box is selected to filter the IPSec traffic in both directions.

    D. Use the TCP port 110

    E. Click Start, click Run, type gpedit.msc, and then click OK.

71. (QID 167) In an FTP's site properties, what directory listing style is recommended for maximum compatibility?

 A. OS2
 B. MS-DOS
 C. WIN 2000
 D. WIN 2003

***E. UNIX**

Explanation: In an FTP's site properties, the UNIX directory listing style is recommended for maximum compatibility. It allows for user running older FTP client software to be able to connect.

---

73. (QID 183) You want to create an IPSec filter list for Terminal Services communications. What steps should you take?

***A. Use the TCP port 80**

 B. Use the TCP port 3389

***C. Verify that the Mirrored check box is selected to filter the IPSec traffic in both directions.**

 D. Use the TCP port 110

***E. Click Start, click Run, type gpedit.msc, and then click OK.**

Explanation: To create an IPSec filter list for Terminal Services communications, click Start, click Run, type gpedit.msc, and then click OK. Expand Security Settings, right-click IP Security Policies, and then click Manage IP filter lists and filter actions. Click the Manage IP Filter Lists tab, and then click Add. Type terminal services in the Name box, and then type for terminal services connections in the Description box. Click to clear the Use Add Wizard check box, and then click Add. Click the Addressing tab, click My IP Address in the Source address box, and then click Any IP Address in the Destination address box.

After you complete this step, the filter is applied to outbound packets. Verify that the Mirrored check box is selected. If this check box is selected, a packet filter is created to match the inbound packets. You must protect all the IPSec-secured communications in both directions. You cannot have IPSec security in only one direction. Click the Protocol tab, click TCP in the Select a protocol box, and then click From this port. Type 3389 in the From this port box, click To any port, and then click OK. Click Close, and then click Close.

72. (QID 178) You need to create a virtual server. How can you accomplish this?

A. Open IIS, expand ServerName where ServerName is the name of the server, right-click Web Sites, point to New, and then click Web Site.

B. The Web Site Creation Wizard starts. Click Next. On the Web Site Description page, type a description for the Web site in the Description box, and then click Next.

C. Select the IP Address, port, host header and path that you want to use for the Web site.

D. Open IIS, expand ServerName where ServerName is the name of the server, right-click Web Sites, point to New, and then click Virtual Server.

E. On the IP Address and Port Settings page, click the IP Address that you want to use for the Web site in the Enter the IP address to use for this Web site box. If you click (All Unassigned), the virtual server responds to all IP addresses that are not assigned to other virtual servers. In effect, this Web site becomes the default Web site. If you want to use a different TCP port than the default TCP port 80, type the port that you want to use in the TCP port this Web site should use (Default 80) box. If you want to specify a host header for the virtual server, type the host header name in the Host Header for this Web site (Default: None) box. Click Next. On the Web Site Home Directory page, specify the path of the Web content folder that you created earlier in the Path box. For example, C:\InetPub\FolderName. If you do not want to allow anonymous access to the Web site, click to clear the Allow anonymous access to this Web site check box, and then click Next. On the Web Site Access Permissions page, specify the permissions that you want for the Web site, and then click Next. Click Finish.

72. (QID 178) You need to create a virtual server. How can you accomplish this?

***A. Open IIS, expand ServerName where ServerName is the name of the server, right-click Web Sites, point to New, and then click Web Site.**
***B. The Web Site Creation Wizard starts. Click Next. On the Web Site Description page, type a description for the Web site in the Description box, and then click Next.**
***C. Select the IP Address, port, host header and path that you want to use for the Web site.**

D. Open IIS, expand ServerName where ServerName is the name of the server, right-click Web Sites, point to New, and then click Virtual Server.

***E. On the IP Address and Port Settings page, click the IP Address that you want to use for the Web site in the Enter the IP address to use for this Web site box. If you click (All Unassigned), the virtual server responds to all IP addresses that are not assigned to other virtual servers. In effect, this Web site becomes the default Web site. If you want to use a different TCP port than the default TCP port 80, type the port that you want to use in the TCP port this Web site should use (Default 80) box. If you want to specify a host header for the virtual server, type the host header name in the Host Header for this Web site (Default: None) box. Click Next. On the Web Site Home Directory page, specify the path of the Web content folder that you created earlier in the Path box. For example, C:\InetPub\FolderName. If you do not want to allow anonymous access to the Web site, click to clear the Allow anonymous access to this Web site check box, and then click Next. On the Web Site Access Permissions page, specify the permissions that you want for the Web site, and then click Next. Click Finish.**

Explanation: To create a virtual server, click Start, point to Administrative Tools, and then click Internet Information Services (IIS) Manager. In the console tree, expand ServerName where ServerName is the name of the server, right-click Web Sites, point to New, and then click Web Site. The Web Site Creation Wizard starts. Click Next. On the Web Site Description page, type a description for the Web site in the Description box, and then click Next. On the IP Address and Port Settings page, click the IP Address that you want to use for the Web site in the Enter the IP address to use for this Web site box. If you click (All Unassigned), the virtual server responds to all IP addresses that are not assigned to other virtual servers.

In effect, this Web site becomes the default Web site. If you want to use a different TCP port than the default TCP port 80, type the port that you want to use in the TCP port this Web site should use (Default 80) box. If you want to specify a host header for the virtual server, type the host header name in the Host Header for this Web site (Default: None) box. Click Next. On the Web Site Home Directory page, specify the path of the Web content folder that you created earlier in the Path box. For example, C:\InetPub\FolderName. If you do not want to allow anonymous access to the Web site, click to clear the Allow anonymous access to this Web site check box, and then click Next. On the Web Site Access Permissions page, specify the permissions that you want for the Web site, and then click Next. Click Finish.

Managing and Maintaining a Server Environment

The objective of this chapter is to provide the reader with an understanding of the following:

4.1 Monitor and analyze events.

> **4.1.1 Tools might include:**
>> 4.1.1.1 Event Viewer
>>
>> 4.1.1.2 System Monitor

4.2 Manage software update infrastructure

4.3 Manage software site licensing

4.4 Manage servers remotely

> **4.4.1 Manage a server by using Remote Assistance**
>
> **4.4.2 Manage a server by using Terminal Services remote administration mode**
>
> **4.4.3 Manage a server by using available support tools**

4.5 Troubleshoot print queues

4.6 Monitor system performance

4.7 Monitor file and print servers. Tools might include:

> **4.7.1 Task Manager**
>> 4.7.1.1 Monitor disk quotas
>>
>> 4.7.1.2 Monitor print queues
>>
>> 4.7.1.3 Monitor server hardware for bottlenecks
>
> **4.7.2 Event Viewer**
>> 4.7.2.1 Monitor disk quotas
>>
>> 4.7.2.2 Monitor print queues
>>
>> 4.7.2.3 Monitor server hardware for bottlenecks
>
> **4.7.3 System Monitor**
>> 4.7.3.1 Monitor disk quotas
>>
>> 4.7.3.2 Monitor print queues
>>
>> 4.7.3.3 Monitor server hardware for bottlenecks

4.8 Monitor and optimize a server environment for application performance

> **4.8.1 Monitor memory performance objects**
>
> **4.8.2 Monitor network performance objects**
>
> **4.8.3 Monitor process performance objects**
>
> **4.8.4 Monitor disk performance objects**

4.9 Manage a Web server

> **4.9.1 Manage Internet Information Services (IIS)**
>
> **4.9.2 Manage security for IIS**

Chapter 4: The Server Environment

1. (QID 168) You need to allow your clients to automatically obtain an IP address, but they don't seem to get addresses on the same network as your domain controller server (it is on the 192.168.10 network). You check one of the client's computers and you find that they have an address that begins with 169.254. What is the first action should you take to resolve this?

    A. Install WINS on your clients

    B. Install WINS on your domain controller

    C. Install DHCP on your domain controller

    D. Install DNS on your clients

2. (QID 169) What steps do you need to take after installing DHCP to ensure that it will provide users with IP addresses in your network?

    A. Configure a scope

    B. Slate a scope

    C. Start the DHCP service

    D. Authorize the DHCP server

    E. Change the IP address of the DHCP server to a dynamic one

1. (QID 168) You need to allow your clients to automatically obtain an IP address, but they don't seem to get addresses on the same network as your domain controller server (it is on the 192.168.10 network). You check one of the client's computers and you find that they have an address that begins with 169.254. What is the first action should you take to resolve this?

    A. Install WINS on your clients
    B. Install WINS on your domain controller
***C. Install DHCP on your domain controller**
    D. Install DNS on your clients

Explanation: To install DHCP in Windows Server 2003, Click Start, click Settings, and then click Control Panel. Double-click Add or Remove Programs, and then click Add/Remove Windows Components. In the Windows Component Wizard, click Networking Services in the Components box, and then click Details. Click to select the Dynamic Host Configuration Protocol (DHCP) check box if it is not already selected, and then click OK. In the Windows Components Wizard, click Next to start Windows Server 2003 Setup. Insert the Windows Server 2003 Advanced Server CD-ROM into your computer's CD-ROM or DVD-ROM drive if you are prompted to do so. Setup copies the DHCP server and tool files to your computer. When Setup is complete, click Finish.

---

2. (QID 169) What steps do you need to take after installing DHCP to ensure that it will provide users with IP addresses in your network?

***A. Configure a scope**
    B. Slate a scope
***C. Start the DHCP service**
***D. Authorize the DHCP server**
    E. Change the IP address of the DHCP server to a dynamic one

Explanation: After installing DHCP, the service must be configured and authorized. When you install and configure DHCP on a domain controller, the server is typically authorized when you add it to the DHCP console. When you install and configure the DHCP service on a member server or stand-alone server, it must be authorized.

3. (QID 170) You configure a scope for your newly installed DHCP service. Users are complaining that they aren't receiving IP addresses from the DHCP server. What should you do?

A. Reinstall the DHCP service

B. Authorize the DHCP server

C. Install WINS

D. Install RRAS

4. (QID 171) You need to restart your DHCP service. Which of the following commands allows you to do this?

A. net boot dhcpserver

B. net stop dhcpserver

C. net start dhcpserver

D. net kick dhcpserver

E. net begin dhcpserver

3. (QID 170) You configure a scope for your newly installed DHCP service. Users are complaining that they aren't receiving IP addresses from the DHCP server. What should you do?

    A. Reinstall the DHCP service

***B. Authorize the DHCP server**

    C. Install WINS

    D. Install RRAS

Explanation: To authorize a DHCP server, click Start, click Programs, click Administrative Tools, and then click DHCP. Select the new DHCP server. If there is a red arrow in the lower-right corner of the server object, the server has not yet been authorized. Right-click the server, and then click Authorize. After a few moments, right-click the server again, and then click Refresh. There should be a green arrow in the lower-right corner to indicate that the server has been authorized.

---

4. (QID 171) You need to restart your DHCP service. Which of the following commands allows you to do this?

    A. net boot dhcpserver

    B. net stop dhcpserver

***C. net start dhcpserver**

    D. net kick dhcpserver

    E. net begin dhcpserver

Explanation: If you need to restart the DHCP service, click Start, click Run, type cmd, and then press ENTER. Type net stop dhcpserver, and then press ENTER. Type net start dhcpserver, and then press ENTER.

5. (QID 172) If you need to create a subnet on a 2003 domain controller, which of the following options will allow you to do so?

A. Start the Active Directory Sites and Services Microsoft Management Console (MMC) snap-in. Double-click the Sites container. Right-click the Subnets container. Click New Subnet. In the Address field, type the Internet Protocol (IP) address and mask that you want to use. Select a site object for this subnet. Click OK.

B. Start the Active Directory Users and Computers Microsoft Management Console (MMC) snap-in. Double-click the Sites container. Right-click the Subnets container. Click New Subnet. In the Address field, type the Internet Protocol (IP) address and mask that you want to use. Select a site object for this subnet. Click OK.

C. Start the Active Directory Domains and Trusts Microsoft Management Console (MMC) snap-in. Double-click the Sites container. Right-click the Subnets container. Click New Subnet. In the Address field, type the Internet Protocol (IP) address and mask that you want to use. Select a site object for this subnet. Click OK.

D. Start the Active Directory Sites and Services Microsoft Management Console (MMC) snap-in. Double-click the Domain Controllers container. Right-click the Subnets container. Click New Subnet. In the Address field, type the Internet Protocol (IP) address and mask that you want to use. Select a site object for this subnet. Click OK.

---

6. (QID 173) You need to deny disk space to users who go beyond their quota limit on the J: drive. How can you accomplish this?

A. Right-click the J: volume that you want to manage and select Properties. Click the Tools tab. Click to select the Deny disk space to users exceeding their quota limit check box. Click OK.

B. Double-click the J: volume that you want to manage and select Properties. Click the Quota tab. Click to select the Deny disk space to users exceeding their quota limit check box. Click OK.

C. Right-click the J: volume that you want to manage and select Properties. Click the Quota tab. Click to select the Deny disk space to users exceeding their quota limit check box. Click OK.

D. Right-click the J: volume that you want to manage and select Properties. Click the General tab. Click to select the Deny disk space to users exceeding their quota limit check box. Click OK.

5. (QID 172) If you need to create a subnet on a 2003 domain controller, which of the following options will allow you to do so?

***A. Start the Active Directory Sites and Services Microsoft Management Console (MMC) snap-in. Double-click the Sites container. Right-click the Subnets container. Click New Subnet. In the Address field, type the Internet Protocol (IP) address and mask that you want to use. Select a site object for this subnet. Click OK.**

B. Start the Active Directory Users and Computers Microsoft Management Console (MMC) snap-in. Double-click the Sites container. Right-click the Subnets container. Click New Subnet. In the Address field, type the Internet Protocol (IP) address and mask that you want to use. Select a site object for this subnet. Click OK.

C. Start the Active Directory Domains and Trusts Microsoft Management Console (MMC) snap-in. Double-click the Sites container. Right-click the Subnets container. Click New Subnet. In the Address field, type the Internet Protocol (IP) address and mask that you want to use. Select a site object for this subnet. Click OK.

D. Start the Active Directory Sites and Services Microsoft Management Console (MMC) snap-in. Double-click the Domain Controllers container. Right-click the Subnets container. Click New Subnet. In the Address field, type the Internet Protocol (IP) address and mask that you want to use. Select a site object for this subnet. Click OK.

Explanation: To create a subnet with Windows 2003 Server, start the Active Directory Sites and Services Microsoft Management Console (MMC) snap-in. Double-click the Sites container. Right-click the Subnets container. Click New Subnet. In the Address field, type the Internet Protocol (IP) address and mask that you want to use. Select a site object for this subnet. Click OK.

6. (QID 173) You need to deny disk space to users who go beyond their quota limit on the J: drive. How can you accomplish this?

A. Right-click the J: volume that you want to manage and select Properties. Click the Tools tab. Click to select the Deny disk space to users exceeding their quota limit check box. Click OK.

B. Double-click the J: volume that you want to manage and select Properties. Click the Quota tab. Click to select the Deny disk space to users exceeding their quota limit check box. Click OK.

***C. Right-click the J: volume that you want to manage and select Properties. Click the Quota tab. Click to select the Deny disk space to users exceeding their quota limit check box. Click OK.**

D. Right-click the J: volume that you want to manage and select Properties. Click the General tab. Click to select the Deny disk space to users exceeding their quota limit check box. Click OK.

Explanation: To prevent users who exceed their assigned quota limit from continuing to write additional data to the volume, click Start, and then click My Computer. Right-click the volume that you want to manage, and then click Properties. Click the Quota tab. Click to select the Deny disk space to users exceeding their quota limit check box. Click OK.

7. (QID 174) You need to log when a user exceeds their disk quota on the X: drive. How can you accomplish this?

A. Double-click the X: volume and select Properties. Click the General tab. You can either click to select the Log event when a user exceeds their quota limit check box or click to select the Log event when a user exceeds their warning level check box. Click OK.

B. Right-click the X: volume and select Properties. Click the Quota tab. You can either click to select the Log event when a user exceeds their quota limit check box or click to select the Log event when a user exceeds their warning level check box. Click OK.

C. Right-click the X: volume and select Properties. Click the Tools tab. You can either click to select the Log event when a user exceeds their quota limit check box or click to select the Log event when a user exceeds their warning level check box. Click OK.

D. Double-click the X: volume and select Properties. Click the Tools tab. You can either click to select the Log event when a user exceeds their quota limit check box or click to select the Log event when a user exceeds their warning level check box. Click OK.

---

8. (QID 177) How would you create a Web content folder called Content in 2003 Server while maintaining a high level of security?

A. Create the Web content folder on the C: drive.

B. Create the Web content folder on the G: drive and enable NTFS permissions.

C. Start My Computer. In the Folders list, click the folder where you want to create the new folder. On the File menu, point to New, and then click Folder. Type the name for the folder as Webcontent, and then press Enter.

D. Start Windows Explorer. In the Folders list, click the folder where you want to create the new folder. On the File menu, point to New, and then click Folder. Type the name for the folder as Content, and then press Enter.

7. (QID 174) You need to log when a user exceeds their disk quota on the X: drive. How can you accomplish this?

A. Double-click the X: volume and select Properties. Click the General tab. You can either click to select the Log event when a user exceeds their quota limit check box or click to select the Log event when a user exceeds their warning level check box. Click OK.

***B. Right-click the X: volume and select Properties. Click the Quota tab. You can either click to select the Log event when a user exceeds their quota limit check box or click to select the Log event when a user exceeds their warning level check box. Click OK.**

C. Right-click the X: volume and select Properties. Click the Tools tab. You can either click to select the Log event when a user exceeds their quota limit check box or click to select the Log event when a user exceeds their warning level check box. Click OK.

D. Double-click the X: volume and select Properties. Click the Tools tab. You can either click to select the Log event when a user exceeds their quota limit check box or click to select the Log event when a user exceeds their warning level check box. Click OK.

Explanation: To log an event to the System log in Event Viewer when a user goes beyond their warning level or quota limit, click Start, and then click My Computer. Right-click the volume that you want to manage, and then click Properties. Click the Quota tab. You can either click to select the Log event when a user exceeds their quota limit check box or click to select the Log event when a user exceeds their warning level check box. Click OK.

---

8. (QID 177) How would you create a Web content folder called Content in 2003 Server while maintaining a high level of security?

A. Create the Web content folder on the C: drive.

***B. Create the Web content folder on the G: drive and enable NTFS permissions.**

C. Start My Computer. In the Folders list, click the folder where you want to create the new folder. On the File menu, point to New, and then click Folder. Type the name for the folder as Webcontent, and then press Enter.

***D. Start Windows Explorer. In the Folders list, click the folder where you want to create the new folder. On the File menu, point to New, and then click Folder. Type the name for the folder as Content, and then press Enter.**

Explanation: To create a new folder where you can store the content for the Web site, start Windows Explorer. In the Folders list, click the folder where you want to create the new folder (i.e. - Inetpub). On the File menu, point to New, and then click Folder. Type a name for the folder, and then press Enter. To provide the maximum level of security, do not create the Web content folder in the root folder of the hard drive.

9. (QID 214) If you don't have the money to add more RAM and you are using Windows 2003, what are some other options for addressing out of memory messages?

A. Decrease the temporary file size in your applications

B. Increase the temporary file size in your applications

C. Increase the paging file size

D. Decrease the paging file size

---

10. (QID 215) What should be done about multiple page faults?

A. Add another CPU to your server

B. Add more memory to your server

C. Add a KVM switch to your server

D. Add more hard drives to your server

9. (QID 214) If you don't have the money to add more RAM and you are using Windows 2003, what are some other options for addressing out of memory messages?

    A. Decrease the temporary file size in your applications

***B. Increase the temporary file size in your applications**

***C. Increase the paging file size**

    D. Decrease the paging file size

Explanation: If you don't have the money to add more RAM and you are using Windows 2003, you can address out of memory messages by either increasing the paging file size (do this with the Advanced tab in the System applet in Control Panel) or increasing the temporary file size in your applications.

---

10. (QID 215) What should be done about multiple page faults?

    A. Add another CPU to your server

***B. Add more memory to your server**

    C. Add a KVM switch to your server

    D. Add more hard drives to your server

Explanation: Add more memory to your server when experiencing multiple page faults.

11. (QID 179) One of your users has a Windows 98 machine and needs access to a HP printing device to which your 2003 print server is connected. What can you do to allow the user to print to the HP printing device?

A. In Printers and Faxes, right-click the printer and then click Properties. With the Sharing tab selected, click Additional Drivers. Click to select the check boxes for the drivers that you want to add. Click OK twice.

B. In Printers and Faxes, double-click the printer and then click Properties. With the Sharing tab selected, click Additional Drivers. Click to select the check boxes for the drivers that you want to add. Click OK twice.

C. In Printers and Faxes, right-click the printer and then click Open. With the Sharing tab selected, click Additional Drivers. Click to select the check boxes for the drivers that you want to add. Click OK twice.

D. In Printers and Faxes, double-click the printer and then click Open. With the Sharing tab selected, click Extra Drivers. Click to select the check boxes for the drivers that you want to add. Click OK twice.

---

12. (QID 180) Which of the following options should you choose if you want to set up a TCP/IP printer in 2003 Server?

A. Make it a network printer

B. Make it a local printer

C. Use a serial port for the printing device

D. Use a USB port for the printing device

E. Choose Standard TCP/IP port and assign an address

11. (QID 179) One of your users has a Windows 98 machine and needs access to a HP printing device to which your 2003 print server is connected. What can you do to allow the user to print to the HP printing device?

***A. In Printers and Faxes, right-click the printer and then click Properties. With the Sharing tab selected, click Additional Drivers. Click to select the check boxes for the drivers that you want to add. Click OK twice.**

    B. In Printers and Faxes, double-click the printer and then click Properties. With the Sharing tab selected, click Additional Drivers. Click to select the check boxes for the drivers that you want to add. Click OK twice.

    C. In Printers and Faxes, right-click the printer and then click Open. With the Sharing tab selected, click Additional Drivers. Click to select the check boxes for the drivers that you want to add. Click OK twice.

    D. In Printers and Faxes, double-click the printer and then click Open. With the Sharing tab selected, click Extra Drivers. Click to select the check boxes for the drivers that you want to add. Click OK twice.

Explanation: With additional printer drivers on your print server, users do not have to download drivers specific to their version of Windows before they can print. To install additional printer drivers, click Start, and then click Printers and Faxes. Right-click the printer for which you want to add additional drivers, and then click Properties. Click the Sharing tab, and then click Additional Drivers. Click to select the check boxes for the drivers that you want to add. Click OK two times.

---

12. (QID 180) Which of the following options should you choose if you want to set up a TCP/IP printer in 2003 Server?

    A. Make it a network printer

***B. Make it a local printer**

    C. Use a serial port for the printing device

    D. Use a USB port for the printing device

***E. Choose Standard TCP/IP port and assign an address**

Explanation: To set up a TCP/IP Printer in Windows 2003 Server, click Start, and then click Printers and Faxes. Double-click Add Printer. In the Add Printer Wizard, click Next. Click Local printer attached to this computer, click to clear the Automatically Detect and Install my Plug and Play Printer check box, and then click Next. Click Create a New Port, click Standard TCP/IP Port in the list, and then click Next. In the Standard TCP/IP Printer Port Wizard, click Next. Type the Internet Protocol (IP) address or the Domain Name System (DNS) name of the network-interface print device, and then click Next. Click Finish. On the Install Printer Software page, click the manufacturer and model of the printer, and then click Next. Type a name for the printer, and then click Next. Click Do not share this printer, and then click Next. Type a location and comment (this step is optional), and then click Next. Click Next. Click Finish.

13. (QID 181) You attempt to set up a Remote Assistance session by clicking the link in an invitation sent to you by one of the company's employees. You find that the Start Remote Assistance isn't available. What do you need to do to fix this?

A. With Internet Explorer open, select the Internet Options in the Tools menu. With the Security tab selected, click Trusted sites, and then click Sites. In the Add this Web site to the zone box and then click Add. Click OK.

B. Click Internet, and then click Custom Level. Under Active scripting, click Enable, and then click OK. Click Yes when you are prompted to change security settings, and then click OK.

C. Reinstall Internet Explorer

D. Update your ActiveX controls

14. (QID 182) You need to install the Windows Terminal Services, Remote Desktop Connection client from a Windows 2003 Server. You have Terminal Services running on the 2003 Server. What steps do you need to take?

A. Share the Client Setup Folder.

B. Share the Server Setup Folder.

C. Install the 32-Bit Terminal Services Client

D. Install the 16-Bit Terminal Services Client

13. (QID 181) You attempt to set up a Remote Assistance session by clicking the link in an invitation sent to you by one of the company's employees. You find that the Start Remote Assistance isn't available. What do you need to do to fix this?

***A. With Internet Explorer open, select the Internet Options in the Tools menu. With the Security tab selected, click Trusted sites, and then click Sites. In the Add this Web site to the zone box and then click Add. Click OK.**
***B. Click Internet, and then click Custom Level. Under Active scripting, click Enable, and then click OK. Click Yes when you are prompted to change security settings, and then click OK.**
    C. Reinstall Internet Explorer
    D. Update your ActiveX controls

Explanation: When you receive a Remote Assistance invitation, and then click the link that opens the Remote Assistance Web page, you may not be able to continue because the Start Remote Assistance button on the Web page is not available. This issue may occur if the Microsoft Internet Explorer security settings do not make it possible for ActiveX Controls that are downloaded from external pages to run. To fix this problem, start Internet Explorer. On the Tools menu, click Internet Options, and then click the Security tab. Click Trusted sites, and then click Sites. In the Add this Web site to the zone box, type https://www.microsoft.com, and then click Add. Click OK. Click Internet, and then click Custom Level. Under Active scripting, click Enable, and then click OK. Click Yes when you are prompted to change security settings, and then click OK. Return to your Remote Assistance invitation, and then click the link to start a Remote Assistance session.

14. (QID 182) You need to install the Windows Terminal Services, Remote Desktop Connection client from a Windows 2003 Server. You have Terminal Services running on the 2003 Server. What steps do you need to take?

***A. Share the Client Setup Folder.**
    B. Share the Server Setup Folder.
***C. Install the 32-Bit Terminal Services Client**
    D. Install the 16-Bit Terminal Services Client

Explanation: First, you need to share the Client Setup Folder. On the Windows 2003 Server computer that is running Terminal Services, open Windows Explorer, and then locate the following folder: drive:\systemroot\System32\Clients\Tsclient\Win32 where drive is the drive that Windows is installed on and systemroot is the folder that contains the Windows installation files. Right-click the Win32 folder, and then click Sharing and Security. In the win32 Properties dialog box, click Share this folder, and then click OK. Next, you will need to install the 32-Bit Terminal Services Client. On the client computer, connect to the shared client installation folder on the server that is running Terminal Services. Click Start, and then click Run. In the Open, box type \\computername\Tsclient\Win32\Setup.exe, where computername is the computer name of the Windows 2003 Server-based computer with the installation shared folder. Click OK. Install the client following the on-screen instructions.

15. (QID 184) You have a need to use Terminal Services and subsequently you need to reactivate a License Server. What steps should you take to do this?

    A. In the console tree, double-click the license server that you want to reactivate, point to Advanced, and then click Reissue Server.

    B. In the console tree, right-click the license server that you want to reactivate, point to Advanced, and then click Reactivate Server.

    C. After the Licensing Wizard starts, confirm that your name, your phone number (optional), and your e-mail address that are listed under Information Needed are correct, and then click Next.

    D. Open the Licensing Terminal Services window.

16. (QID 185) You need to add some counters to System Monitor. What steps should you take?

    A. Click Start, point to Programs, and then click Performance.

    B. Right-click the System Monitor Details pane, and then click Add Counters.

    C. Click Start, point to Administrative Tools, and then click Performance.

    D. Double-click the System Monitor Details pane, and then click Add Counters.

15. (QID 184) You have a need to use Terminal Services and subsequently you need to reactivate a License Server. What steps should you take to do this?

    A. In the console tree, double-click the license server that you want to reactivate, point to Advanced, and then click Reissue Server.

***B. In the console tree, right-click the license server that you want to reactivate, point to Advanced, and then click Reactivate Server.**

***C. After the Licensing Wizard starts, confirm that your name, your phone number (optional), and your e-mail address that are listed under Information Needed are correct, and then click Next.**

***D. Open the Licensing Terminal Services window.**

Explanation: To reactivate a License Server, open the Licensing Terminal Services window. In the console tree, right-click the license server that you want to reactivate, point to Advanced, and then click Reactivate Server. After the Licensing Wizard starts, confirm that your name, your phone number (optional), and your e-mail address that are listed under Information Needed are correct, and then click Next.

---

16. (QID 185) You need to add some counters to System Monitor. What steps should you take?

    A. Click Start, point to Programs, and then click Performance.

***B. Right-click the System Monitor Details pane, and then click Add Counters.**

***C. Click Start, point to Administrative Tools, and then click Performance.**

    D. Double-click the System Monitor Details pane, and then click Add Counters.

Explanation: If you need to add counters to System Monitor, click Start, point to Administrative Tools, and then click Performance. If you select an object on a remote computer, you may experience a short delay as System Monitor refreshes the list to reflect objects that are present on that computer. Right-click the System Monitor Details pane, and then click Add Counters. To monitor any computer on which the monitoring console is run, click Use local computer counters. Or, to monitor a specific computer regardless of where the monitoring console is run, click Select counters from computer, and then specify a computer name. Under Performance object, click an object to monitor. By default, the Processor object is selected. Click All counters or click Select counters from the list, and then click one of the list items. Click Add.

17. (QID 186) Which of the following counters can monitor your hard disk?

   A. Physical Disk\ Disk Reads/sec

   B. Memory\ Page Reads/sec

   C. LogicalDisk\ % Free Space

   D. Physical Disk\ Disk Writes/sec

   E. Server\ Pool Paged Bytes

---

18. (QID 187) Which of the following counters can monitor your memory?

   A. Network Interface\ Packets/sec

   B. Memory\ Transition Faults/sec

   C. System\Context switches/sec

   D. Memory\ Pages/sec

   E. Memory\ Available Bytes

17. (QID 186) Which of the following counters can monitor your hard disk?

***A. Physical Disk\ Disk Reads/sec**
     B. Memory\ Page Reads/sec
***C. LogicalDisk\ % Free Space**
***D. Physical Disk\ Disk Writes/sec**
     E. Server\ Pool Paged Bytes

Explanation: The following counters can be monitored when you need to observer hard disk performance: Physical Disk\ Disk Reads/sec, Physical Disk\ Disk Writes/sec, and LogicalDisk\ % Free Space.

---

18. (QID 187) Which of the following counters can monitor your memory?

     A. Network Interface\ Packets/sec
***B. Memory\ Transition Faults/sec**
     C. System\Context switches/sec
***D. Memory\ Pages/sec**
***E. Memory\ Available Bytes**

Explanation: The following counters can be monitored when you need to observe memory performance: Memory\ Available Bytes, Memory\ Cache Bytes, Memory\ Pages/sec, Memory\ Page Reads/sec, Memory\ Transition Faults/sec, Memory\ Pool Paged Bytes, and Memory\ Pool Nonpaged Bytes.

19. (QID 188) Which of the following counters can monitor your network performance?

    A. Server\ Bytes Total/sec

    B. System\Context switches/sec

    C. Network Interface\ Bytes total/sec

    D. Server\ Bytes Received/sec

    E. Memory\ Transition Faults/sec

---

20. (QID 189) Which of the following counters can monitor your processor performance?

    A. System\ Processor Queue Length

    B. Server\ Bytes Received/sec

    C. Processor\ % Processor Time

    D. System\Context switches/sec

    E. Memory\ Transition Faults/sec

19. (QID 188) Which of the following counters can monitor your network performance?

***A. Server\ Bytes Total/sec**

    B. System\Context switches/sec

***C. Network Interface\ Bytes total/sec**

***D. Server\ Bytes Received/sec**

    E. Memory\ Transition Faults/sec

Explanation: The following counters can be monitored when you need to observe network performance: Network Interface\ Bytes total/sec, Network Interface\ Packets/sec, Server\ Bytes Total/sec, Server\ Bytes Transmitted/sec, and Server\ Bytes Received/sec.

---

20. (QID 189) Which of the following counters can monitor your processor performance?

***A. System\ Processor Queue Length**

    B. Server\ Bytes Received/sec

***C. Processor\ % Processor Time**

***D. System\Context switches/sec**

    E. Memory\ Transition Faults/sec

Explanation: The following counters can be monitored when you need to observe processor performance: Processor\ % Processor Time, System\ Processor Queue Length, Processor\ Interrupts/sec, and System\Context switches/sec.

21. (QID 190) Which of the following performance counters should be used when you need to measure the number of bytes sent and received per second on a NIC?

    A. Bytes Total / Sec

    B. Average Bytes

    C. Average Queue

    D. Packets Total / Sec

22. (QID 191) What does the Committed Bytes performance counter measure?

    A. How much memory is being used by applications, programs and/or the operating system

    B. How many bytes pass through a network card

    C. How much page file space is being used

    D. How many bits pass through a network card

21. (QID 190) Which of the following performance counters should be used when you need to measure the number of bytes sent and received per second on a NIC?

***A. Bytes Total / Sec**
    B. Average Bytes
    C. Average Queue
    D. Packets Total / Sec

Explanation: The Bytes Total / Sec performance counter should be used when you need to measure the number of bytes sent and received per second on a NIC. Use this performance counter if domain users complain about long log on times at specific periods during the day.

---

22. (QID 191) What does the Committed Bytes performance counter measure?

***A. How much memory is being used by applications, programs and/or the operating system**
    B. How many bytes pass through a network card
***C. How much page file space is being used**
    D. How many bits pass through a network card

Explanation: The Committed Bytes performance counter measures how much memory is being used by applications, programs and/or the operating system as well as how much page file space is being used.

23. (QID 192) What benefits can adding an extra file server produce?

    A. It will help to increase the traffic of the network

    B. It will help to balance the traffic of the network

    C. It will help to lessen the traffic of the network

    D. It will help to change the traffic of the network

---

24. (QID 193) Multiple processors can help in which of the following situations?

    A. When the present processor is handling the load

    B. When using a single-threaded application

    C. When the present processor is overloaded

    D. When using a multi-threaded application

23. (QID 192) What benefits can adding an extra file server produce?

     A. It will help to increase the traffic of the network

***B. It will help to balance the traffic of the network**

     C. It will help to lessen the traffic of the network

     D. It will help to change the traffic of the network

Explanation: Adding an extra file server will help to balance the traffic of the network.

---

24. (QID 193) Multiple processors can help in which of the following situations?

     A. When the present processor is handling the load

     B. When using a single-threaded application

***C. When the present processor is overloaded**

***D. When using a multi-threaded application**

Explanation: Multiple processors can help when using a multi-threaded application or when the present processor is overloaded.

25. (QID 194) Which of the following counters measure the number of threads waiting on the processor?

    A. Server Work Queues: Queue Length

    B. Server Work Queues: % Processor Time

    C. System: Processor Queue Length

    D. System: % Threads

---

26. (QID 195) Which of the following would indicate a disk bottleneck?

    A. If you have an FAT(16) partition

    B. If you have a basic disk that hasn't been imported

    C. If you have a number of I/O request pending on a drive

    D. If you have a basic disk that hasn't been initialized

25. (QID 194) Which of the following counters measure the number of threads waiting on the processor?

***A. Server Work Queues: Queue Length**

    B. Server Work Queues: % Processor Time

***C. System: Processor Queue Length**

    D. System: % Threads

Explanation: The Server Work Queues: Queue Length and the counter measures the number of threads waiting on the processor.

---

26. (QID 195) Which of the following would indicate a disk bottleneck?

    A. If you have an FAT(16) partition

    B. If you have a basic disk that hasn't been imported

***C. If you have a number of I/O request pending on a drive**

    D. If you have a basic disk that hasn't been initialized

Explanation: If you have a number of I/O request pending on a drive, this would indicate a disk bottleneck.

27. (QID 196) You probably need to replace your hard drive if System Monitor indicates which of the following?

    A. Avg. Mem sec/Transfer is 425.2

    B. Average % Processor Time is 87%

    C. Average Pages/Sec 27.322

    D. Network Interface: Bytes Total/sec is 241.322

    E. Avg. Disk sec/Transfer is 3.132

---

28. (QID 197) You probably need to upgrade your processor if System Monitor indicates which of the following?

    A. Average Pages/Sec 27.322

    B. Avg. Disk sec/Transfer is 3.132

    C. Average % Processor Time is 87%

    D. Network Interface:Bytes Total/sec is 241.322

    E. Avg. Mem sec/Transfer is 425.2

27. (QID 196) You probably need to replace your hard drive if System Monitor indicates which of the following?

    A. Avg. Mem sec/Transfer is 425.2
    B. Average % Processor Time is 87%
    C. Average Pages/Sec 27.322
    D. Network Interface: Bytes Total/sec is 241.322
***E. Avg. Disk sec/Transfer is 3.132**

Explanation: An Avg. Disk sec/Transfer of 3.132 would indicate that the hard drive needs to be replaced, since it should be much lower, not even 1.0. An Average % Processor Time of 87% would indicate a need for a processor upgrade. If Average Pages/Sec is 27.322, then more RAM is needed, since the average should be more like 15 or less. Network Interface: Bytes Total/sec is 241.322 this is within the normal parameters for a NIC card.

---

28. (QID 197) You probably need to upgrade your processor if System Monitor indicates which of the following?

    A. Average Pages/Sec 27.322
    B. Avg. Disk sec/Transfer is 3.132
***C. Average % Processor Time is 87%**
    D. Network Interface:Bytes Total/sec is 241.322
    E. Avg. Mem sec/Transfer is 425.2

Explanation: An Avg. Disk sec/Transfer of 3.132 would indicate that the hard drive needs to be replaced, since it should be much lower, not even 1.0. An Average % Processor Time of 87% would indicate a need for a processor upgrade. If Average Pages/Sec is 27.322, then more RAM is needed, since the average should be more like 15 or less. Network Interface: Bytes Total/sec is 241.322 this is within the normal parameters for a NIC card.

29. (QID 198) You probably need to upgrade your RAM if System Monitor indicates which of the following?

A. Average Pages/Sec 27.322

B. Avg. Disk sec/Transfer is 3.132

C. Average % Processor Time is 87%

D. Network Interface: Bytes Total/sec is 241.322

E. Avg. Mem sec/Transfer is 425.2

30. (QID 199) If we want a DHCP server to provide IP and DNS information automatically for a client, what options should be selected in General TCP/IP properties?

A. Use the following DNS server addresses

B. Obtain DNS server address automatically

C. Use the following IP address

D. Obtain an IP address automatically

29. (QID 198) You probably need to upgrade your RAM if System Monitor indicates which of the following?

***A. Average Pages/Sec 27.322**
    B. Avg. Disk sec/Transfer is 3.132
    C. Average % Processor Time is 87%
    D. Network Interface: Bytes Total/sec is 241.322
    E. Avg. Mem sec/Transfer is 425.2

Explanation: An Avg. Disk sec/Transfer of 3.132 would indicate that the hard drive needs to be replaced, since it should be much lower, not even 1.0. An Average % Processor Time of 87% would indicate a need for a processor upgrade. If Average Pages/Sec is 27.322, then more RAM is needed, since the average should be more like 15 or less. Network Interface: Bytes Total/sec is 241.322 this is within the normal parameters for a NIC card.

---

30. (QID 199) If we want a DHCP server to provide IP and DNS information automatically for a client, what options should be selected in General TCP/IP properties?

    A. Use the following DNS server addresses
***B. Obtain DNS server address automatically**
    C. Use the following IP address
***D. Obtain an IP address automatically**

Explanation: If we want a DHCP server to provide IP and DNS information automatically for a client, select the following options: Obtain an IP address automatically & Obtain DNS server address automatically.

31. (QID 200) Which of the following would you use to deploy a service pack?

    A. Update.dll

    B. Update.msi

    C. Update.bat

    D. Update.txt

    E. Update.exe

---

32. (QID 201) Hard page faults are corrected by a/an __________ upgrade.

    A. RAM

    B. Processor

    C. Hard Drive

    D. Operating System

    E. ROM

31. (QID 200) Which of the following would you use to deploy a service pack?

      A. Update.dll
      B. Update.msi
      C. Update.bat
      D. Update.txt
***E. Update.exe**

Explanation: To apply a service pack, use the update.exe utility (scripts are used to install service packs). Update.msi is used when you are assigning something. Batch and text extensions have nothing to do with service packs.

---

32. (QID 201) Hard page faults are corrected by a/an __________ upgrade.

***A. RAM**
      B. Processor
      C. Hard Drive
      D. Operating System
      E. ROM

Explanation: Hard page faults, which are satisfied by the hard drive, are corrected by a RAM upgrade. Processor load is reduced with more RAM and hard page faults decrease.

33. (QID 202) You probably need to replace your hard drive if System Monitor indicates which of the following?

    A. Average Pages/Sec 27.322

    B. Average % Processor Time is 87%

    C. Avg. Disk sec/Transfer is 3.132

    D. Network Interface: Bytes Total/sec is 241.322

    E. Avg. Mem sec/Transfer is 425.2

---

34. (QID 203) You probably need to upgrade your processor if System Monitor indicates which of the following?

    A. Average % Processor Time is 87%

    B. Avg. Disk sec/Transfer is 3.132

    C. Average Pages/Sec 27.322

    D. Network Interface:Bytes Total/sec is 241.322

    E. Avg. Mem sec/Transfer is 425.2

33. (QID 202) You probably need to replace your hard drive if System Monitor indicates which of the following?

    A. Average Pages/Sec 27.322

    B. Average % Processor Time is 87%

***C. Avg. Disk sec/Transfer is 3.132**

    D. Network Interface: Bytes Total/sec is 241.322

    E. Avg. Mem sec/Transfer is 425.2

Explanation: An Avg. Disk sec/Transfer of 3.132 would indicate that the hard drive needs to be replaced, since it should be much lower, not even 1.0. If Average % Processor Time is 87%, this would indicate a need for a processor upgrade. If Average Pages/Sec is 27.322, then more RAM is needed, since the average should be more like 15 or less. Network Interface: Bytes Total/sec is 241.322 and this is within the normal parameters for a NIC card.

---

34. (QID 203) You probably need to upgrade your processor if System Monitor indicates which of the following?

***A. Average % Processor Time is 87%**

    B. Avg. Disk sec/Transfer is 3.132

    C. Average Pages/Sec 27.322

    D. Network Interface:Bytes Total/sec is 241.322

    E. Avg. Mem sec/Transfer is 425.2

Explanation: An Avg. Disk sec/Transfer of 3.132 would indicate that the hard drive needs to be replaced, since it should be much lower, not even 1.0. An Average % Processor Time of 87% would indicate a need for a processor upgrade. If Average Pages/Sec is 27.322, then more RAM is needed, since the average should be more like 15 or less. Network Interface: Bytes Total/sec is 241.322 this is within the normal parameters for a NIC card.

35. (QID 204) You probably need to upgrade your RAM if System Monitor indicates which of the following?

A. Avg. Mem sec/Transfer is 425.2

B. Avg. Disk sec/Transfer is 3.132

C. Average % Processor Time is 87%

D. Network Interface: Bytes Total/sec is 241.322

E. Average Pages/Sec 27.322

---

36. (QID 205) The network segment that your client is on is the 192.168.18 segment. The subnet mask for the network segment is 255.255.255.128 and the router interface for the network segment is 192.168.18.1. The client can't get out of the network segment. The client has an IP address of 192.168.19.5, a subnet mask of 255.255.255.224, and a default gateway of 192.168.17.1. What should you change to allow the client to get out onto the network?

A. Change the IP address to 192.168.18.5. Change the Subnet Mask to 255.255.255.128. Change the Default Gateway to 192.168.18.1.

B. Leave the IP address as it is. Change the Subnet Mask to 255.255.255.128. Change the Default Gateway to 192.168.18.1.

C. Change the IP address to 192.168.18.5. Leave the Subnet Mask as it is. Change the Default Gateway to 192.168.18.1.

D. Change the IP address to 192.168.18.5. Change the Subnet Mask to 255.255.255.128. Leave the Default Gateway as it is.

35. (QID 204) You probably need to upgrade your RAM if System Monitor indicates which of the following?

    A. Avg. Mem sec/Transfer is 425.2
    B. Avg. Disk sec/Transfer is 3.132
    C. Average % Processor Time is 87%
    D. Network Interface: Bytes Total/sec is 241.322

***E. Average Pages/Sec 27.322**

Explanation: An Avg. Disk sec/Transfer of 3.132 would indicate that the hard drive needs to be replaced, since it should be much lower, not even 1.0. An Average % Processor Time of 87% would indicate a need for a processor upgrade. If Average Pages/Sec is 27.322, then more RAM is needed, since the average should be more like 15 or less. Network Interface: Bytes Total/sec is 241.322 this is within the normal parameters for a NIC card.

---

36. (QID 205) The network segment that your client is on is the 192.168.18 segment. The subnet mask for the network segment is 255.255.255.128 and the router interface for the network segment is 192.168.18.1. The client can't get out of the network segment. The client has an IP address of 192.168.19.5, a subnet mask of 255.255.255.224, and a default gateway of 192.168.17.1. What should you change to allow the client to get out onto the network?

***A. Change the IP address to 192.168.18.5. Change the Subnet Mask to 255.255.255.128. Change the Default Gateway to 192.168.18.1.**

    B. Leave the IP address as it is. Change the Subnet Mask to 255.255.255.128. Change the Default Gateway to 192.168.18.1.

    C. Change the IP address to 192.168.18.5. Leave the Subnet Mask as it is. Change the Default Gateway to 192.168.18.1.

    D. Change the IP address to 192.168.18.5. Change the Subnet Mask to 255.255.255.128. Leave the Default Gateway as it is.

Explanation: The network segment that your client is on is the 192.168.18 segment, not the 192.168.19 segment. The subnet mask for the network segment is 255.255.255.128, not 255.255.255.224 and the router interface for the network segment is 192.168.18.1, not 192.168.17.1.

37. (QID 206) When using driver signing options, which of the following options should you choose if you want to prevent installation of unsigned files?

A. Ignore

B. Block

C. Warn

D. Apply setting as system default

---

38. (QID 207) Ideally, where should a paging file be placed in a Windows environment where the server operating system is located on the master hard drive (C:)?

A. On C:\Windows

B. On D: (a separate hard drive)

C. On E: (the CD-ROM drive)

D. Anywhere on C:

37. (QID 206) When using driver signing options, which of the following options should you choose if you want to prevent installation of unsigned files?

    A. Ignore

***B. Block**

    C. Warn

***D. Apply setting as system default**

Explanation: When using driver signing options, you have the following options: Ignore, Warn, and Block. Ignore installs all files, regardless of file signature. Warn displays a message before installing an unsigned file. Block prevents installation of unsigned files. There is also an Administrator option: Apply setting as system default, which is necessary to make changes permanent.

38. (QID 207) Ideally, where should a paging file be placed in a Windows environment where the server operating system is located on the master hard drive (C:)?

    A. On C:\Windows

***B. On D: (a separate hard drive)**

    C. On E: (the CD-ROM drive)

    D. Anywhere on C:

Explanation: Ideally, a paging file should be placed on a separate hard drive from where the server operating system is located (in this example on D:).

39. (QID 208) You are setting up a new server, you unsuccessfully attempt to use the PING utility to contact other servers in the domain. What should you check?

A. Check to see if BIND is being used

B. Check to see if your default gateway is correct

C. Check to see if your subnet mask matches theirs

D. Check to see if WINS is being used.

---

40. (QID 209) Which of the following plans would be the best one to establish a baseline for a server?

A. Use performance monitoring software (i.e. - System Monitor) at the same time daily for a week or so

B. Use performance monitoring software (i.e. - System Monitor) continuously for three days

C. Add more RAM and a better CPU

D. Connect it to a UPS

39. (QID 208) You are setting up a new server, you unsuccessfully attempt to use the PING utility to contact other servers in the domain. What should you check?

    A. Check to see if BIND is being used

***B. Check to see if your default gateway is correct**

***C. Check to see if your subnet mask matches theirs**

    D. Check to see if WINS is being used.

Explanation: You are setting up a new server, you unsuccessfully attempt to use the PING utility to contact other servers in the domain. Check to see if your subnet mask matches theirs and if your default gateway is correct. BIND (UNIX's answer to DNS) and WINS have nothing to do with pinging an IP address.

---

40. (QID 209) Which of the following plans would be the best one to establish a baseline for a server?

***A. Use performance monitoring software (i.e. - System Monitor) at the same time daily for a week or so**

    B. Use performance monitoring software (i.e. - System Monitor) continuously for three days

    C. Add more RAM and a better CPU

    D. Connect it to a UPS

Explanation: Use performance monitoring software (i.e. - System Monitor) at the same time daily for a week or so will establish a baseline for a server.

41. (QID 210) How can you change your network identification in Windows 2003?

    A. Go to Device Manager

    B. Go to System Properties

    C. Go to Network Properties

    D. Go to Network and dial up connections

---

42. (QID 211) If you want to map a drive letter in Windows 2003, how can you do it?

    A. Use Device Manager

    B. Use Control Panel

    C. Right-click My Computer

    D. Right-click My Network Places

41. (QID 210) How can you change your network identification in Windows 2003?

    A. Go to Device Manager

***B. Go to System Properties**

    C. Go to Network Properties

    D. Go to Network and dial up connections

Explanation: By right-clicking on My Computer and selecting Properties, we can bring up System Properties. Here we can access the Network Identification tab.

---

42. (QID 211) If you want to map a drive letter in Windows 2003, how can you do it?

    A. Use Device Manager

    B. Use Control Panel

***C. Right-click My Computer**

***D. Right-click My Network Places**

Explanation: If you want to map a drive letter in Windows 2003, right-click either the My Computer icon or the My Network Places icon and select the map network drive option.

43. (QID 212) If you want to join a domain and you have Windows 2003 on your computer, how would you accomplish this?

    A. Right-click the My Computer icon, and select manage. Then, select the Network Identification tab.

    B. Right-click the My Network Places icon, and select properties. Then, select the Network Identification tab.

    C. Right-click the My Network Places icon, and select manage. Then, select the Network Identification tab.

    D. Right-click the My Computer icon, and select properties. Then, select the Network Identification tab.

---

44. (QID 213) How can you see resources used by a device in Windows 2003?

    A. Go to the Start Menu button, and choose the Run option. Type in WINMSD.EXE and click OK.

    B. Go to the Start Menu button, then to All Programs, Accessories, System Tools, and System Information.

    C. Right-click the My Computer option and select properties. Select the Hardware tab and choose Device Manager.

    D. Right-click the My Network Places option and select properties. Select the Hardware tab and choose Device Manager.

43. (QID 212) If you want to join a domain and you have Windows 2003 on your computer, how would you accomplish this?

    A. Right-click the My Computer icon, and select manage. Then, select the Network Identification tab.

    B. Right-click the My Network Places icon, and select properties. Then, select the Network Identification tab.

    C. Right-click the My Network Places icon, and select manage. Then, select the Network Identification tab.

***D. Right-click the My Computer icon, and select properties. Then, select the Network Identification tab.**

Explanation: If you want to join a domain and you have Windows 2003 on your computer, right-click the My Computer icon, and select properties (System Properties). Then, select the Network Identification tab.

---

44. (QID 213) How can you see resources used by a device in Windows 2003?

***A. Go to the Start Menu button, and choose the Run option. Type in WINMSD.EXE and click OK.**

***B. Go to the Start Menu button, then to All Programs, Accessories, System Tools, and System Information.**

***C. Right-click the My Computer option and select properties. Select the Hardware tab and choose Device Manager.**

    D. Right-click the My Network Places option and select properties. Select the Hardware tab and choose Device Manager.

Explanation: If you want to view resources used by a device in Windows 2003, use System Information or Device Manager. To access System Information, use one of the following methods: go to the Start Menu button, and choose the Run option. type in WINMSD.EXE and click OK or you can go to the Start Menu button, then to All Programs, Accessories, System Tools, and System Information. To access Device Manager, right-click the My Computer option and select properties. Select the Hardware tab and choose Device Manager.

45. (QID 175) How would you configure IIS to use Microsoft .NET Passport authentication?

A. In IIS Manager, expand Server_name, where Server_name is the name of the server, and then expand Web Sites.

B. In the console tree, right-click the Web site, virtual directory, or file for which you want to configure authentication, and then click Properties. Click the Directory Security or File Security tab (as appropriate), and then under Anonymous and access control, click Edit.

C. Click to select the check box next to the Microsoft .NET Passport authentication method.

D. In the console tree, double-click the Web site, virtual directory, or file for which you want to configure authentication, and then click Properties. Click the Directory Security or File Security tab (as appropriate), and then under Anonymous and access control, click Open.

45. (QID 175) How would you configure IIS to use Microsoft .NET Passport authentication?

***A. In IIS Manager, expand Server_name, where Server_name is the name of the server, and then expand Web Sites.**
***B. In the console tree, right-click the Web site, virtual directory, or file for which you want to configure authentication, and then click Properties. Click the Directory Security or File Security tab (as appropriate), and then under Anonymous and access control, click Edit.**
***C. Click to select the check box next to the Microsoft .NET Passport authentication method.**

> D. In the console tree, double-click the Web site, virtual directory, or file for which you want to configure authentication, and then click Properties. Click the Directory Security or File Security tab (as appropriate), and then under Anonymous and access control, click Open.

Explanation: To configure authentication in IIS, start IIS Manager or open the IIS snap-in. Expand Server_name, where Server_name is the name of the server, and then expand Web Sites. In the console tree, right-click the Web site, virtual directory, or file for which you want to configure authentication, and then click Properties. Click the Directory Security or File Security tab (as appropriate), and then under Anonymous and access control, click Edit. Click to select the check box next to the authentication method or methods that you want to use, and then click OK. The authentication methods that are set by default are Anonymous access and Integrated Windows authentication. When anonymous access is turned on, no authenticated user credentials are required to access the site. This option is best used when you want to grant public access to information that requires no security.

When a user tries to connect to your Web site, IIS assigns the connection to the IUSER_ComputerName account, where ComputerName is the name of the server on which IIS is running. By default, the IUSER_ComputerName account is a member of the Guests group. This group has security restrictions, imposed by NTFS file system permissions that designate the level of access and the type of content that is available to public users. To edit the Windows account used for anonymous access, click Browse in the Anonymous access box. Integrated Windows authentication (this used to be NTLM or Windows NT Challenge/Response authentication) sends user authentication information over the network as a Kerberos ticket, and provides a high level of security. Windows Integrated authentication uses Kerberos version 5 and NTLM authentication. To use this method, clients must use Microsoft Internet Explorer 2.0 or later.

Additionally, Windows Integrated authentication is not supported over HTTP proxy connections. This option is best used for an intranet, where both the user and Web server computers are in the same domain, and administrators can make sure that every user is using Internet Explorer 2.0 or later. Digest authentication requires a user ID and password, provides a medium level of security, and may be used when you want to grant access to secure information from public networks. This method offers the same functionality as basic authentication. However, this method transmits user credentials across the network as an MD5 hash, or message digest, in which the original user name and password cannot be deciphered from the hash.

To use this method, clients must use Microsoft Internet Explorer 5.0 or later, and the Web clients and Web servers must be members of, or be trusted by, the same domain. If you turn on digest authentication, type the realm name in the Realm box.

Basic authentication requires a user ID and password, and provides a low level of security. User credentials are sent in clear text across the network. This format provides a low level of security because almost all protocol analyzers can read the password. However, it is compatible with the widest number of Web clients. This option is best used when you want to grant access to information with little or no need for privacy. If you turn on basic authentication, type the domain name that you want to use in the Default domain box. You can also optionally enter a value in the Realm box. Microsoft .NET Passport authentication provides single sign-in security, which provides users with access to diverse services on the Internet. When you select this option, requests to IIS must contain valid .NET Passport credentials on either the query string or in the cookie. If IIS does not detect .NET Passport credentials, requests are redirected to the .NET Passport logon page. You can also limit access based on source IP address, source network ID, or source domain name.

---

10. (QID 176) Which of the following methods of authentication are available in IIS 6.0 for 2003 Server?

   A. Integrated Windows authentication

   B. Digest authentication

   C. Dual authentication

   D. Microsoft .NET Passport authentication

46. (QID 176) Which of the following methods of authentication are available in IIS 6.0 for 2003 Server?

***A. Integrated Windows authentication**
***B. Digest authentication**
***C. Dual authentication**
  D. Microsoft .NET Passport authentication

Explanation: To configure authentication in IIS, start IIS Manager or open the IIS snap-in. Expand Server_name, where Server_name is the name of the server, and then expand Web Sites. In the console tree, right-click the Web site, virtual directory, or file for which you want to configure authentication, and then click Properties. Click the Directory Security or File Security tab (as appropriate), and then under Anonymous and access control, click Edit. Click to select the check box next to the authentication method or methods that you want to use, and then click OK. The authentication methods that are set by default are Anonymous access and Integrated Windows authentication. When anonymous access is turned on, no authenticated user credentials are required to access the site. This option is best used when you want to grant public access to information that requires no security.

When a user tries to connect to your Web site, IIS assigns the connection to the IUSER_ComputerName account, where ComputerName is the name of the server on which IIS is running. By default, the IUSER_ComputerName account is a member of the Guests group.

This group has security restrictions, imposed by NTFS file system permissions that designate the level of access and the type of content that is available to public users. To edit the Windows account used for anonymous access, click Browse in the Anonymous access box. Integrated Windows authentication (this used to be NTLM or Windows NT Challenge/Response authentication) sends user authentication information over the network as a Kerberos ticket, and provides a high level of security. Windows Integrated authentication uses Kerberos version 5 and NTLM authentication. To use this method, clients must use Microsoft Internet Explorer 2.0 or later.

Additionally, Windows Integrated authentication is not supported over HTTP proxy connections. This option is best used for an intranet, where both the user and Web server computers are in the same domain, and administrators can make sure that every user is using Internet Explorer 2.0 or later. Digest authentication requires a user ID and password, provides a medium level of security, and may be used when you want to grant access to secure information from public networks. This method offers the same functionality as basic authentication. However, this method transmits user credentials across the network as an MD5 hash, or message digest, in which the original user name and password cannot be deciphered from the hash. To use this method, clients must use Microsoft Internet Explorer 5.0 or later, and the Web clients and Web servers must be members of, or be trusted by, the same domain. If you turn on digest authentication, type the realm name in the Realm box. Basic authentication requires a user ID and password, and provides a low level of security. User credentials are sent in clear text across the network. This format provides a low level of security because the password can be read by almost all protocol analyzers. However, it is compatible with the widest number of Web clients. This option is best used when you want to grant access to information with little or no need for privacy. If you turn on basic authentication, type the domain name that you want to use in the Default domain box. You can also optionally enter a value in the Realm box. Microsoft .NET Passport authentication provides single sign-in security, which provides users with access to diverse services on the Internet. When you select this option, requests to IIS must contain valid .NET Passport credentials on either the query string or in the cookie.

If IIS does not detect .NET Passport credentials, requests are redirected to the .NET Passport logon page. You can also limit access based on source IP address, source network ID, or source domain name.

Managing and Implementing Disaster Recovery

The objective of this chapter is to provide the reader with an understanding of the following:

5.1 Perform system recovery for a server

    5.1.1 Implement Automated System Recovery (ASR)

    5.1.2 Restore data from shadow copy volumes

    5.1.3 Back up files and System State data to media

    5.1.4 Configure security for backup operations

5.2 Manage backup procedures

    5.2.1 Verify the successful completion of backup jobs

    5.2.2 Manage backup storage media

5.3 Recover from server hardware failure

5.4 Restore backup data

5.5 Schedule backup jobs

Chapter 5: Disaster Recovery

1. (QID 216) In what instances would using shadow copies be helpful?

   A. You need to convert back to FAT32

   B. You accidentally overwrite a file

   C. Your Server 2003 OS kernel is corrupted

   D. Recovery of files that were accidentally deleted

---

2. (QID 217) Which of the following executables starts the Volume Shadow Copy service?

   A. Vscadmin.exe

   B. Vssadmin.exe

   C. Sssadmin.exe

   D. Vsscopy.exe

1. (QID 216) In what instances would using shadow copies be helpful?

     A. You need to convert back to FAT32

***B. You accidentally overwrite a file**

     C. Your Server 2003 OS kernel is corrupted

***D. Recovery of files that were accidentally deleted**

Explanation: The Shadow Copies feature provides point-in-time copies of files on network shares. With shadow copies of shared folders, you can view the contents of network folders as they existed at points of time in the past. This is very helpful if you want to recover files that were accidentally deleted. This is the network equivalent of the Recycle Bin functionality. If you accidentally delete a file, you can open an old version of the file, and then copy it to a safe location. Shadow copies of shared folders can recover files that are deleted by any mechanism, as long as the required history folder exists. Do you want to recover a file after you accidentally overwrite it?

Shadow copies of shared folders can be very useful in environments where you commonly create new files by opening an existing file, making modifications, and then saving the file with a new name. You can use a shadow copy of the shared folder to recover the previous version of the file. Do you want to check different versions of the same file while you are working on the file? You could use shadow copies of shared folders during the normal work cycle when you want to determine what has changed between two versions of the same file. For example, you might want to see what your original text looked like before you spent time editing the file.

2. (QID 217) Which of the following executables starts the Volume Shadow Copy service?

     A. Vscadmin.exe

***B. Vssadmin.exe**

     C. Sssadmin.exe

     D. Vsscopy.exe

Explanation: You can access shadow copies of shared folders on the Shadow Copies tab of the Local Disk Properties dialog box. You can also view the same dialog box in the Computer Management snap-in. To do so, right-click Shares, point to All Tasks, and then click Configure Shadow Copies. The Vssadmin.exe tool is the command-line equivalent tool for the Volume Shadow Copy service.

3. (QID 218) How can you access shadow copies in 2003 Server?

A. In Device Manager, right-click Shares, point to All Tasks, and then click Configure Shadow Copies.

B. With the Copies tab of the Local Disk Properties dialog box.

C. In Computer Management, right-click Shares, point to All Tasks, and then click Configure Shadow Copies.

D. With the Shadow Copies tab of the Local Disk Properties dialog box.

---

4. (QID 219) Which of the following NTBACKUP parameters allows you to back up the system state data?

A. systemstate

B. bks file name

C. bksfl name

D. ssdata

3. (QID 218) How can you access shadow copies in 2003 Server?

    A. In Device Manager, right-click Shares, point to All Tasks, and then click Configure Shadow Copies.

    B. With the Copies tab of the Local Disk Properties dialog box.

***C. In Computer Management, right-click Shares, point to All Tasks, and then click Configure Shadow Copies.**

***D. With the Shadow Copies tab of the Local Disk Properties dialog box.**

Explanation: You can access shadow copies of shared folders on the Shadow Copies tab of the Local Disk Properties dialog box. You can also view the same dialog box in the Computer Management snap-in. To do so, right-click Shares, point to All Tasks, and then click Configure Shadow Copies. The Vssadmin.exe tool is the command-line equivalent tool of the Volume Shadow Copy service.

---

4. (QID 219) Which of the following NTBACKUP parameters allows you to back up the system state data?

***A. systemstate**

    B. bks file name

    C. bksfl name

    D. ssdata

Explanation: The systemstate parameter indicates that you want to back up the system state data. The bks file name parameter indicates the name of the backup selection file (.bks file) to be used for the backup operation. The /j switch indicates the job name to be used in the log file. The /p switch indicates the media pool from which you want to use media (you can't use the /a /g /f /t switches with this switch). The /g switch overwrites or appends to this tape. The /t switch overwrites or appends to this tape. The /n switch indicates the new tape name and can't be used with the /a switch. The /f switch indicates the logical disk path and file name and it cannot be used with the /p /g /t switches. The /d switch indicates a label for each backup set. The /a switch performs an append operation and the /g or /t must be used with this switch, but not with the /p switch.

The /v switch verifies the data after the backup is complete. The /r switch restricts access to this tape for the owner or members of the Administrators group. The /l:{f|s|n} switch indicates the type of log file: f=full, s=summary, n=none (with n, no log file is created). The /m switch indicates the backup type (normal, copy, differential, incremental, or daily). The /rs switch backs up the Removable Storage database. The /hc:{on|off} switch uses hardware compression on the tape drive. The /um switch locates the first available media, formats it, and uses it for the current backup operation.

5. (QID 220) Which of the following NTBACKUP parameters indicates the name of the backup selection file?

    A. ssdata

    B. systemstate

    C. bksfl name

    D. bks file name

    E. job name

---

6. (QID 221) Which of the following NTBACKUP switches verifies the data after the backup is complete?

    A. The /a switch

    B. The /r switch

    C. The /v switch

    D. The /m switch

    E. The /t switch

5. (QID 220) Which of the following NTBACKUP parameters indicates the name of the backup selection file?

>A. ssdata
>B. systemstate
>C. bksfl name
>***D. bks file name**
>E. job name

---

6. (QID 221) Which of the following NTBACKUP switches verifies the data after the backup is complete?

>A. The /a switch
>B. The /r switch
>***C. The /v switch**
>D. The /m switch
>E. The /t switch

Explanation: The systemstate parameter indicates that you want to back up the system state data. The bks file name parameter indicates the name of the backup selection file (.bks file) to be used for the backup operation. The /j switch indicates the job name to be used in the log file. The /p switch indicates the media pool from which you want to use media (you can't use the /a /g /f /t switches with this switch). The /g switch overwrites or appends to this tape. The /t switch overwrites or appends to this tape. The /n switch indicates the new tape name and can't be used with the /a switch. The /f switch indicates the logical disk path and file name and it cannot be used with the /p /g /t switches. The /d switch indicates a label for each backup set.

The /a switch performs an append operation and the /g or /t must be used with this switch, but not with the /p switch. The /v switch verifies the data after the backup is complete. The /r switch restricts access to this tape for the owner or members of the Administrators group. The /l:{flsln} switch indicates the type of log file: f=full, s=summary, n=none (with n, no log file is created). The /m switch indicates the backup type (normal, copy, differential, incremental, or daily). The /rs switch backs up the Removable Storage database. The /hc:{onloff} switch uses hardware compression on the tape drive. The /um switch locates the first available media, formats it, and uses it for the current backup operation.

7. (QID 222) Which of the following NTBACKUP switches restricts access to a tape for the owner or members of the Administrators group?

    A. The /l switch

    B. The /v switch

    C. The /r switch

    D. The /m switch

    E. The /e switch

---

8. (QID 223) When used with the NTBACKUP command, the /l switch can indicate what log file types?

    A. e=edit

    B. f=full

    C. n=none

    D. p=partial

    E. s=summary

7. (QID 222) Which of the following NTBACKUP switches restricts access to a tape for the owner or members of the Administrators group?

> A. The /I switch
> B. The /v switch

***C. The /r switch**

> D. The /m switch
> E. The /e switch

8. (QID 223) When used with the NTBACKUP command, the /l switch can indicate what log file types?

> A. e=edit

***B. f=full**

***C. n=none**

> D. p=partial

***E. s=summary**

Explanation: The systemstate parameter indicates that you want to back up the system state data. The bks file name parameter indicates the name of the backup selection file (.bks file) to be used for the backup operation. The /j switch indicates the job name to be used in the log file. The /p switch indicates the media pool from which you want to use media (you can't use the /a /g /f /t switches with this switch). The /g switch overwrites or appends to this tape. The /t switch overwrites or appends to this tape. The /n switch indicates the new tape name and can't be used with the /a switch. The /f switch indicates the logical disk path and file name and it cannot be used with the /p /g /t switches. The /d switch indicates a label for each backup set.

The /a switch performs an append operation and the /g or /t must be used with this switch, but not with the /p switch. The /v switch verifies the data after the backup is complete. The /r switch restricts access to this tape for the owner or members of the Administrators group. The /l:{flsln} switch indicates the type of log file: f=full, s=summary, n=none (with n, no log file is created). The /m switch indicates the backup type (normal, copy, differential, incremental, or daily). The /rs switch backs up the Removable Storage database. The /hc:{on|off} switch uses hardware compression on the tape drive. The /um switch locates the first available media, formats it, and uses it for the current backup operation.

9. (QID 224) When used with the NTBACKUP command, the /m switch can indicate what type of backup is performed. What types of backup are available with the /m switch?

A. Normal

B. Partial

C. Daily

D. Differential

E. Supplemental

10. (QID 225) When used with the NTBACKUP command, what does the /um switch do?

A. Locates the first available tape drive

B. Locates the first available hard drive

C. Formats the first available media

D. Uses the first available media for the current backup operation

E. Locates the first available media

9. (QID 224) When used with the NTBACKUP command, the /m switch can indicate what type of backup is performed. What types of backup are available with the /m switch?

***A. Normal**
    B. Partial
***C. Daily**
***D. Differential**
    E. Supplemental

---

10. (QID 225) When used with the NTBACKUP command, what does the /um switch do?

    A. Locates the first available tape drive
    B. Locates the first available hard drive
***C. Formats the first available media**
***D. Uses the first available media for the current backup operation**
***E. Locates the first available media**

Explanation: The systemstate parameter indicates that you want to back up the system state data. The bks file name parameter indicates the name of the backup selection file (.bks file) to be used for the backup operation. The /j switch indicates the job name to be used in the log file. The /p switch indicates the media pool from which you want to use media (you can't use the /a /g /f /t switches with this switch). The /g switch overwrites or appends to this tape. The /t switch overwrites or appends to this tape. The /n switch indicates the new tape name and can't be used with the /a switch. The /f switch indicates the logical disk path and file name and it cannot be used with the /p /g /t switches. The /d switch indicates a label for each backup set.

The /a switch performs an append operation and the /g or /t must be used with this switch, but not with the /p switch. The /v switch verifies the data after the backup is complete. The /r switch restricts access to this tape for the owner or members of the Administrators group. The /l:{f|s|n} switch indicates the type of log file: f=full, s=summary, n=none (with n, no log file is created). The /m switch indicates the backup type (normal, copy, differential, incremental, or daily). The /rs switch backs up the Removable Storage database. The /hc:{on|off} switch uses hardware compression on the tape drive. The /um switch locates the first available media, formats it, and uses it for the current backup operation.

11. (QID 226) How do you create an ASR floppy disk from an ASR backup set in Windows 2003 Server?

A. Start the backup wizard

B. Reboot and enter safe mode, edit the Asrpnp.sif file

C. Copy the Asrpnp.sif file to the A: drive

D. Start the ASR wizard

E. Copy the Asr.sif file to the A: drive

12. (QID 227) You attempt to restore a RAID 5 array on your 2003 Server box. However, when you attempt to run ASR, you get the following error message: Logical Disk Manager ASR Utility Error. The Logical Disk Manager encountered the following error while restoring the dynamic disk configuration on this system: Failed to commit the disk group creation transaction. Additional information: -25- . What is the cause of this error message?

A. ASR cannot be used with RAID arrays

B. One of the disks in the array is missing or corrupted.

C. ASR cannot be used with RAID-5 arrays

D. The disk needs to be defragmented first before using ASR

11. (QID 226) How do you create an ASR floppy disk from an ASR backup set in Windows 2003 Server?

***A. Start the backup wizard**

    B. Reboot and enter safe mode, edit the Asrpnp.sif file

***C. Copy the Asrpnp.sif file to the A: drive**

    D. Start the ASR wizard

***E. Copy the Asr.sif file to the A: drive**

Explanation: Insert a blank, pre-formatted floppy disk into your computer's floppy drive. Click Start, point to All Programs, point to Accessories, point to System Tools, and then click Backup. The Backup Wizard starts. Click Advanced Mode. On the Welcome tab, click Restore Wizard (Advanced). The Restore Wizard starts. Click Next. On the What to Restore page, click to select the check box next to the media that contains the ASR backup. Expand the ASR backup set that corresponds to the ASR floppy disk that you want to create.

Expand the second instance of the drive letter that contains the system files, expand Windows_Folder, and then expand the Repair folder. In the right pane, click to select the check boxes next to Asr.sif and Asrpnp.sif, and then click Next. On the Completing the Restore Wizard page, click Advanced. On the Where to Restore page, click Single Folder in the Restore files to box, type A:\ in the Folder name box, and then click Next. Follow the instructions on the remaining pages of the wizard.

12. (QID 227) You attempt to restore a RAID 5 array on your 2003 Server box. However, when you attempt to run ASR, you get the following error message: Logical Disk Manager ASR Utility Error. The Logical Disk Manager encountered the following error while restoring the dynamic disk configuration on this system: Failed to commit the disk group creation transaction. Additional information: -25- . What is the cause of this error message?

    A. ASR cannot be used with RAID arrays

***B. One of the disks in the array is missing or corrupted.**

    C. ASR cannot be used with RAID-5 arrays

    D. The disk needs to be defragmented first before using ASR

Explanation: When you use Automated System Recovery (ASR) to restore disks that are in a redundant array of independent disks (RAID) set on a computer, you may receive the following error message: Logical Disk Manager ASR Utility Error. The Logical Disk Manager encountered the following error while restoring the dynamic disk configuration on this system: Failed to commit the disk group creation transaction. Additional information: -25- . This behavior may occur if there are corrupted or missing disks in the configuration.

13. (QID 228) What is the correct path to set up a restore point in Windows 2003 Server?

    A. Start | Programs | System Tools | Accessories | System Restore

    B. Start | Programs | Accessories | Communication Tools | System Restore.

    C. Start | Programs | Accessories | System Tools | Disk Cleanup.

    D. Start | Programs | Accessories | Tools | System Restore.

    E. Start | Programs | Accessories | System Tools | System Restore

---

14. (QID 229) System Restore will create restore points before which of the following events?

    A. Driver installs

    B. AutoUpdate installations

    C. Rebuild boor process

    D. Restorations operations

    E. Application installations that are System Restore compliant

13. (QID 228) What is the correct path to set up a restore point in Windows 2003 Server?

    A. Start | Programs | System Tools | Accessories | System Restore

    B. Start | Programs | Accessories | Communication Tools | System Restore.

    C. Start | Programs | Accessories | System Tools | Disk Cleanup.

    D. Start | Programs | Accessories | Tools | System Restore.

***E. Start | Programs | Accessories | System Tools | System Restore**

Explanation: To set up a restore point in Windows 2003 Server, go to Start | Programs | Accessories | System Tools | System Restore.

---

14. (QID 229) System Restore will create restore points before which of the following events?

    A. Driver installs

***B. AutoUpdate installations**

    C. Rebuild boor process

***D. Restorations operations**

***E. Application installations that are System Restore compliant**

Explanation: System Restore will automatically create a restore point before application installations that are System Restore compliant, AutoUpdate installations, and restoration operations.

15. (QID 230) Which of the following can be restored using System Restore?

   A. Registry

   B. SAM Hives

   C. The IIS Metabase

   D. The COM+ database

   E. Contents of redirected folders

---

16. (QID 231) Which of the following scenarios is correct for using Last Known Good with System Restore if your 2003 server won't boot?

   A. Just use Last Known Good; it won't work with System Restore

   B. Just use System Restore; it won't work with Last Known Good

   C. First, use the Last Known Good method to get the computer to boot and then use System Restore to get the previous state that you want.

   D. Use System Restore and then use Last Known Good to get the state you want

15. (QID 230) Which of the following can be restored using System Restore?

***A. Registry**

    B. SAM Hives

***C. The IIS Metabase**

***D. The COM+ database**

    E. Contents of redirected folders

Explanation: System Restore can restore the Registry, local profiles, the COM+ database, WFP.dll cache, the WMI database, and the IIS Metabase.

---

16. (QID 231) Which of the following scenarios is correct for using Last Known Good with System Restore if your 2003 server won't boot?

    A. Just use Last Known Good; it won't work with System Restore

    B. Just use System Restore; it won't work with Last Known Good

***C. First, use the Last Known Good method to get the computer to boot and then use System Restore to get the previous state that you want.**

    D. Use System Restore and then use Last Known Good to get the state you want

Explanation: Last Known Good should be used when there is a non-bootable state. Once booted into either SafeMode or Normal Mode, System Restore can be used to capture optimal previous state. System Restore cannot be accessed unless the system is bootable into one of these modes.

17. (QID 232) Which of the following statements are true regarding how System Restore works with drivers?

    A. If unsigned drivers cause problems, you can revert to the restore point before the bad driver was installed

    B. If signed drivers cause problems, you can revert to the restore point before the bad driver was installed

    C. If signed drivers cause problems, there isn't a restore point created specifically before the bad signed driver was installed

    D. If unsigned drivers cause problems, there isn't a restore point created specifically before the bad signed driver was installed

---

18. (QID 235) Which of the following commands can you run if the Dllcache folder becomes damaged?

    A. sfc /redocache

    B. sfc /fixcache

    C. sfc /purgecache

    D. sfc /cache

    E. sfc /scanedit

17. (QID 232) Which of the following statements are true regarding how System Restore works with drivers?

***A. If unsigned drivers cause problems, you can revert to the restore point before the bad driver was installed**

    B. If signed drivers cause problems, you can revert to the restore point before the bad driver was installed

***C. If signed drivers cause problems, there isn't a restore point created specifically before the bad signed driver was installed**

    D. If unsigned drivers cause problems, there isn't a restore point created specifically before the bad signed driver was installed

Explanation: Using System Restore, if an unsigned driver installation appears to be the source of undesired system behavior, users can revert their systems to the restore point created automatically just before a driver was installed. In the event the device driver was signed, System Restore would not create a restore point. However, the effects of that device driver installation can still be reverted using System Restore, by restoring to the most recently created restore point before the driver was installed. This will revert changes made to the system by the driver, as well as any changes made after that restore point was created.

---

18. (QID 235) Which of the following commands can you run if the Dllcache folder becomes damaged?

    A. sfc /redocache
    B. sfc /fixcache

***C. sfc /purgecache**

    D. sfc /cache
    E. sfc /scanedit

Explanation: System File Checker, sfc, is a command-line tool that scans and verifies the versions of all protected system files after you restart your computer. If the Dllcache folder becomes damaged or unusable, use sfc with the /purgecache switch to repair its contents.

19. (QID 234) Which of the following system files does Windows File Protection protect?

A. SYS

B. ASC

C. BAT

D. DLL

E. EXE

---

20. (QID 233) What steps have to be accomplished with ASR before you can use System Restore?

A. Boot recovery process

B. Rebuild boor process

C. Registry edit

D. COM+ edit

E. OS restore process

19. (QID 234) Which of the following system files does Windows File Protection protect?

***A. SYS**
    B. ASC
    C. BAT
***D. DLL**
***E. EXE**

Explanation: Windows File Protection prevents the replacement of protected system files, such as .sys, .dll, .ocx, .ttf, .fon, and .exe files. Windows File Protection is a component that runs in the background and protects all files that are installed by the Windows Setup program.

---

20. (QID 233) What steps have to be accomplished with ASR before you can use System Restore?

***A. Boot recovery process**
    B. Rebuild boor process
    C. Registry edit
    D. COM+ edit
***E. OS restore process**

Explanation: Automated System Recovery (ASR) extends conventional backup-and-restore applications by providing a framework for saving and recovering the Windows XP operating state, in the event of a catastrophic system or hardware failure. Windows XP ASR recovers the target system in a two-step process. The first step, termed the boot recovery process, requires a new copy of Windows XP to be temporarily installed on the target system using the original distribution media. The second step, called the OS restore process, restores the files of a previously saved Windows XP installation using a backup-and-restore application (thus deleting and writing over some of the files installed by the boot recovery process).

In the event of a system failure, the ASR can be used to restart the system, after which users can begin a recovery from a backed up copy of a previously saved Windows XP installation. While System Restore is useful to undo harmful changes to system files, the system must be bootable to either SafeMode or Normal Mode for System Restore to restore these changes. In the event of catastrophic failure, with ASR and a conventional backup-and-recovery application, users can boot the system using the original media and then recover a backed-up previous Windows XP installation.

Once a system is recovered, previous System Restore restore points will no longer be available, nor will the restore points associated with the recovered installation. A fully-recovered system via ASR will restart System Restore's monitoring and restore point creation capabilities, just as an upgrade or reinstall of the operating system.

21. (QID 236) You need to start a system file check on your 2003 Server. Which of the following commands will allow you to do this?

    B. sfc /scan

    C. sfc /sc

    D. sfc /startscan

    E. sfc /scannow

22. (QID 237) You need to run signature verification of your Windows 2003 Server. What is the proper procedure to do this?

    A. Click Start, select the Run option, type sigvrf and then click OK.

    B. Click Start, select the Run option, type sigverif and then click OK.

    C. Click Start, select the Run option, type sigv and then click OK.

    D. Click Start, select the Run option, type sigverifnow and then click OK.

21. (QID 236) You need to start a system file check on your 2003 Server. Which of the
    following commands will allow you to do this?

      B. sfc /scan
      C. sfc /sc
      D. sfc /startscan

***E. sfc /scannow**

Explanation: To start a system file check, click Start, click Run, and then typesfc
/scannow.

---

22. (QID 237) You need to run signature verification of your Windows 2003 Server.
    What is the proper procedure to do this?

      A. Click Start, select the Run option, type sigvrf and then click OK.

***B. Click Start, select the Run option, type sigverif and then click OK.**

      C. Click Start, select the Run option, type sigv and then click OK.
      D. Click Start, select the Run option, type sigverifnow and then click OK.

Explanation: To start File Signature Verification, click Start, click Run, type sigverif
and then click OK.

23. (QID 238) You have two serial devices on the same IRQ and conflicts are occurring. What action should you take?

A. Change the DMA of one of the devices

B. Change the IRQ of one of the devices

C. Change the memory address of one of the devices

D. Change the I/O address of one of the devices

---

24. (QID 239) After noting the properties of the installed device driver, which of the following steps should you take when updating device drivers on a Windows 2003 server?

A. Note the properties of the updated driver, and install the new driver

B. Test the new driver on a non-critical machine, note the properties of the updated driver, and install the new driver

C. Simply install the new driver

D. Install the new driver and rollback if necessary

23. (QID 238) You have two serial devices on the same IRQ and conflicts are occurring. What action should you take?

      A. Change the DMA of one of the devices
***B. Change the IRQ of one of the devices**
      C. Change the memory address of one of the devices
      D. Change the I/O address of one of the devices

Explanation: If you have two devices on the same IRQ, you should change the IRQ for one of the devices, otherwise conflicts can occur.

---

24. (QID 239) After noting the properties of the installed device driver, which of the following steps should you take when updating device drivers on a Windows 2003 server?

      A. Note the properties of the updated driver, and install the new driver
***B. Test the new driver on a non-critical machine, note the properties of the updated driver, and install the new driver**
      C. Simply install the new driver
      D. Install the new driver and rollback if necessary

Explanation: After noting the properties of the installed device driver, test the new driver on a non-critical machine, note the properties of the updated driver, and install the new driver.

25. (QID 240) If a user tells you that they aren't able to log on their computer after installing a hardware device and it gave them the STOP message, what course of action would require the least effort?

    A. Restarting by using safe mode

    B. Performing a brand-new install of the operating system

    C. Restarting with the last known good configuration

    D. Restarting with the Windows 2003 CD-ROM and using Recovery Console

26. (QID 241) If a Windows 2003 Server displays a STOP message a few times after having a NIC card installed on it, what would be the quickest way to access files on the 2003 Server?

    A. Safe Mode

    B. Device Manager

    C. Emergency Repair Disk

    D. Recovery Console

    E. Last Known Good Configuration

25. (QID 240) If a user tells you that they aren't able to log on their computer after installing a hardware device and it gave them the STOP message, what course of action would require the least effort?

    A. Restarting by using safe mode
    B. Performing a brand-new install of the operating system
***C. Restarting with the last known good configuration**
    D. Restarting with the Windows 2003 CD-ROM and using Recovery Console

Explanation: The option that requires the least effort in this scenario is the last known good configuration. Safe mode would be next in line as far as effort is concerned. Recovery Console and performing a brand-new install would require a great deal of effort.

---

26. (QID 241) If a Windows 2003 Server displays a STOP message a few times after having a NIC card installed on it, what would be the quickest way to access files on the 2003 Server?

***A. Safe Mode**
    B. Device Manager
    C. Emergency Repair Disk
    D. Recovery Console
    E. Last Known Good Configuration

Explanation: Safe mode won't load network drivers, so the bad drivers installed with the NIC won't negatively affect the machine. This is the fastest way to get the files. It is quicker than last known good configuration and Recovery Console. An Emergency Repair Disk doesn't apply.

27. (QID 242) If you receive multiple stop messages after having installed a new hardware device each time you rebooted, which of the following method would you want to use to get the computer back up and running as soon as possible?

   A. Safe mode

   B. Device Manager

   C. Recovery Console

   D. Parallel Installation

   E. Last Known Good Configuration

---

28. (QID 243) What is an incremental backup?

   A. It is generally done just once a month

   B. It is a backup in which only files that have increased in size are backed up.

   C. It is a normal backup

   D. It is not used as a daily backup method

27. (QID 242) If you receive multiple stop messages after having installed a new hardware device each time you rebooted, which of the following method would you want to use to get the computer back up and running as soon as possible?

***A. Safe mode**
    B. Device Manager
    C. Recovery Console
    D. Parallel Installation
    E. Last Known Good Configuration

Explanation: Safe mode would be the quickest choice since bad drivers are the root of the problem. Last Known Good Configuration can't be used since multiple stop messages have come up. Using Recovery Console or a Parallel Installation to repair the installation would take a while.

---

28. (QID 243) What is an incremental backup?

    A. It is generally done just once a month
***B. It is a backup in which only files that have increased in size are backed up.**
    C. It is a normal backup
    D. It is not used as a daily backup method

Explanation: The incremental backup method is a backup where only files that have increased in size are backed up. It is generally done daily and to restore fully you would need all incremental since the last normal backup and the normal backup itself.

29. (QID 244) When using a normal and differential backup method, how many tapes will be required to restore the server?

A. 1 tapes

B. 2 tapes

C. 3 tapes

D. 4 tapes

E. 8 tapes

---

30. (QID 245) When you need to reduce the time spent backing up the system while maintaining a relatively quick backup time, what backup method should you implement?

A. Use only incrementals

B. Use a normal backup once a week and incrementals the rest of the week

C. Use only normal backups

D. Use a normal backup once a week and differentials the rest of the week

29. (QID 244) When using a normal and differential backup method, how many tapes will be required to restore the server?

***A. 1 tapes**
    B. 2 tapes
    C. 3 tapes
    D. 4 tapes
    E. 8 tapes

Explanation: When using a normal and differential backup method, two tapes will be required to restore the server. The normal backup tape catches everything, and the differential tape catches the difference since the last full backup tape.

---

30. (QID 245) When you need to reduce the time spent backing up the system while maintaining a relatively quick backup time, what backup method should you implement?

    A. Use only incrementals
    B. Use a normal backup once a week and incrementals the rest of the week
    C. Use only normal backups
***D. Use a normal backup once a week and differentials the rest of the week**

Explanation: When you need to reduce the time spent backing up the system while maintaining a relatively quick backup time, use a normal backup once a week and differentials the rest of the week. This accomplishes both goals. The other solutions either take too long to restore or too long to backup.

31. (QID 246) Which of the following backup methods allows for the lowest possibility of data loss?

    A. A normal backup every week and daily differentials

    B. A normal backup every week and daily incrementals

    C. A normal backup every week

    D. Incremental backups only

---

32. (QID 247) What is true of using a backup method that uses a weekly normal and daily incrementals?

    A. It requires less time for restoration

    B. It requires more time for restoration

    C. It increases the daily backup time

    D. It minimizes the daily backup time

---

33. (QID 248) How can you install Recovery Console on a hard drive with Windows 2003?

    A. Use the winnt32.exe command with the /cmdcons switch

    B. Use the winnt32.exe command by itself

    C. Use the winnt.exe command with the /cmdcons switch

    D. Use the winnt32.exe command by itself

31. (QID 246) Which of the following backup methods allows for the lowest possibility of data loss?

***A. A normal backup every week and daily differentials**
    B. A normal backup every week and daily incrementals
    C. A normal backup every week
    D. Incremental backups only

Explanation: A normal backup every week and daily differentials allows for the least amount of data loss, since the differential catches everything since the last normal backup and you only need the most recent differential tape and the most recent normal backup. If you used incrementals, they would all be necessary and if one of them went bad, you could only restore up to that tape.

32. (QID 247) What is true of using a backup method that uses a weekly normal and daily incrementals?

 A. It requires less time for restoration
***B. It requires more time for restoration**
    C. It increases the daily backup time
***D. It minimizes the daily backup time**

Explanation: The backup method that uses a weekly normal and daily incrementals minimizes the daily backup time and it requires more time for restoration.

33. (QID 248) How can you install Recovery Console on a hard drive with Windows 2003?

***A. Use the winnt32.exe command with the /cmdcons switch**
    B. Use the winnt32.exe command by itself
    C. Use the winnt.exe command with the /cmdcons switch
    D. Use the winnt32.exe command by itself

Explanation: Use the winnt32.exe command with the /cmdcons switch if you want to install Recovery Console on a hard drive with Windows 2003.

Notes:

Online Exams
Home   About Us   Contact Us   Faqs/Help   My Home
Home
Returning User
Corporate User
New User
Buy an Exam / Membership
Free Sample Exam
- copyright -
- disclaimer -
- privacy -
- site map -
- terms of use -
Welcome to the new online-exams.com!
Welcome back to Online-Exams.com
You are in the right place to select from 45 tests and over 16,000 relevant questions across six technology certifications. Online-exams.com is an industry leader in I.T. training. Purchase just one test at a time for US $5 or choose a monthly membership starting at US $19 for greater savings.
To purchase an exam:
• Click one of the links on the top left of your screen to begin: returning, corporate or new user.
Free sample:
• Click here to try a sample exam
Available content:
• Our content offering includes: CheckPoint, Cisco, Citrix, CIW / Web, CompTIA and Microsoft.
Prefer hard-copy content?
• If you prefer award-winning content in book format, why not visit our partner at www.ebooster.co.uk - take advantage of free shipping in Europe and Asia!
Safe & secure
Sensitive information you exchange with us is secured using GeoTrust site certificates. Click below for details:
E-mail the webmaster
© 1996-2004

TotalRecall Gives You *Four* Levels of Computer Certification Practice Exams, Books, and eBooks

- Study formats and prices vary so you can choose one that best fits your level of knowledge and skills.
- Each format offers you either free or discounted access to our popular BeachFront Quizzer test engine. See description below.
- ALL come with our exclusive Money-Back Guarantee—pass the exam your first time or get money back!

1. InsideScoop Certification Success Series

Paperback books in the InsideScoop series offer a package of comprehensive study manual and CD-ROM of the BeachFront Quizzer test engine with answers/ explanations linked to relevant chapters in an integrated eBook. The study manual includes detailed information about each core exam topic with pre/post assessment quizzes; an abundance of figures, diagrams and photos; chapter summaries; helpful tips and time management techniques for test taking; lists of useful websites, articles and other learning resources; and an extensive glossary of 600 computer, IT, and telecommunications terms.

Paperback Books are $89.99

2. InsidersChoice Certification Success Series

Paperback books in the InsidersChoice series offer a package of comprehensive study manual and FREE download of the BeachFront Quizzer test engine with answers/ explanations linked to relevant chapters in an integrated eBook. The study manual includes detailed information about each core exam topic with pre/post assessment quizzes; an abundance of figures, diagrams and photos; chapter summaries; helpful tips and time management techniques for test taking; lists of useful websites, articles and other learning resources; and an extensive glossary of 600 computer, IT, and telecommunications terms.

Paperbacks are $59.99 and eBooks are $44.99

3. ExamInsight IT Certification System Series

Paperback books and eBooks in the ExamInsight series offer a package of compact study guide and 50% discount to purchase a download of the BeachFront Quizzer test engine with answers/ explanations linked to relevant chapters in an integrated eBook. The study guide includes compact information about each core exam topic with pre/post assessment quizzes; an abundance of figures, diagrams and photos; chapter summaries; helpful tips and time management techniques for test taking; and lists of useful websites, articles and other learning resources

Paperbacks are $39.99 and eBooks are $29.99

4. ExamWise IT Question Book Series

Paperback books and eBooks in the ExamWise series offer a package of Q&A workbook and 30-Day FREE access to a BeachFront Quizzer online practice exam. Each ExamWise Q&A workbook offers you approximately 300 practice questions organized by core exam topic. Questions are arranged in a unique format of two questions per right and page, with answers and brief explanations on the reverse page.

Paperbacks are $39.99 and eBooks are $29.99

The BeachFront Quizzer Test Engine Makes Passing Certification Exams as Easy as a Day at the Beach...

The BeachFront Quizzer test engine was pioneered in 1995 by Bruce Moran, an ex-NASA IT professional turned vocational computer instructor and certification trainer before launching his own book publishing operation in 2002. This popular test engine introduced interactive and adaptive features that other publishers have since tried to imitate, but never duplicate. It offers you four helpful study formats:

1) Adaptive technology generates 15-25 questions in 30-minute sessions to help you identify your strengths and weaknesses for each exam topic.

2) Study sessions help strengthen your weakest exam topics by generating up to 250 questions per topic until you can answer each correctly. Explanations for each question are linked to relevant chapters in an eBook study manual and often to web sites to help you develop a complete understanding of why an answer is correct. By focusing on your rough spots, we'll get you certified fast—guaranteed or get money back!

3) Simulated exams generate randomized questions about core exam topics in 60-90 minute sessions and then provide a score summary by topic. Taking multiple practice exams will build your confidence and ability to concentrate during the real deal!

4) Flash card drills present questions to answer mentally and then allow you to click F4 to display the correct answer.

Visit our web sites for more information:

www.TotalRecallPress.com   /   www.bfq.com

TotalRecall Certification Publications Microsoft

InsideScoop: TotalRecall's Complete Certification System Series:

InsideScoop to MCP / MCSE Certification: Exam 70-210
Managing Microsoft Windows 2000 Professional

InsideScoop to MCP / MCSE Certification: **Exam 70-216**
Implementing and Administering a Microsoft Windows 2000 Network Infrastructure

InsideScoop to MCP / MCSE Certification: **Exam 70-217**
Managing a Microsoft Directory Services Infrastructure

InsideScoop to MCP / MCSE Certification: **Exam 70-219**
Designing a Windows 2000 Directory Services Infrastructure

InsideScoop to MCP / MCSE Certification: **Exam 70-220**
Designing Security for a Microsoft Windows 2000 Network

InsideScoop to MCP / MCSE Certification: **Exam 70-221**
Designing a Microsoft Windows 2000 Network Infrastructure

InsideScoop to MCP / MCSE Certification: **Exam 70-227**
Installing, Configuring, and Administering Microsoft Internet Security
and Acceleration (ISA) Server 2000, Enterprise Edition

InsideScoop to MCP / MCSE Certification: **Exam 70-270**
Installing, Configuring, and Administering Microsoft Windows XP Professional

InsideScoop to MCP / MCSE Certification: **Exam 70-290**
Managing and Maintaining a Microsoft Windows Server 2003 Environment

InsideScoop to MCP / MCSE Certification: **Exam 70-291**
Managing, and Maintaining a Microsoft Windows Server 2003 Network Infrastructure

InsideScoop to MCP / MCSE Certification: **Exam 70-292**
Managing and Maintaining a Microsoft Windows Server 2003
Environment for an MCSA Certified on Windows 2000

InsideScoop to MCP / MCSE Certification: **Exam 70-293**
Planning and Maintaining a Microsoft Windows Server 2003 Network Infrastructure

InsideScoop to MCP / MCSE Certification: **Exam 70-294**
Plan and Maintain a Microsoft Windows Server 2003 Active Directory Infrastructure

InsideScoop to MCP / MCSE Certification: **Exam 70-296**
Planning, Implementing, and Maintaining a Microsoft Windows Server 2003
Environment for an MCSE Certified on Windows

InsideScoop to MCP / MCSE Certification: **Exam 70-297**
Designing Microsoft Windows Server 2003 Active Directory and Network Infrastructure

InsideScoop to MCP / MCSE Certification: **Exam 70-298**
Designing Security for a Microsoft Server 2003 Network

InsideScoop to MCP / MCSE Certification: **Exam 70-299**
Implementing and Administering Security in a Microsoft Windows Server 2003 Network

ExamInsight: TotalRecall IT Insight Certification Book Series:

ExamInsight For MCP / MCSE Certification:　　　　　　　　**Exam 70-210**
Managing Microsoft Windows 2000 Professional

ExamInsight For MCP / MCSE Certification:　　　　　　　　**Exam 70-216**
Implementing and Administering a Microsoft Windows 2000 Network Infrastructure

ExamInsight For MCP / MCSE Certification:　　　　　　　　**Exam 70-217**
Managing a Microsoft Directory Services Infrastructure

ExamInsight For MCP / MCSE Certification:　　　　　　　　**Exam 70-219**
Designing a Windows 2000 Directory Services Infrastructure

ExamInsight For MCP / MCSE Certification:　　　　　　　　**Exam 70-220**
Designing Security for a Microsoft Windows 2000 Network

ExamInsight For MCP / MCSE Certification:　　　　　　　　**Exam 70-221**
Designing a Microsoft Windows 2000 Network Infrastructure

ExamInsight For MCP / MCSE Certification:　　　　　　　　**Exam 70-227**
Installing, Configuring, and Administering Microsoft Internet Security
and Acceleration (ISA) Server 2000, Enterprise Edition

ExamInsight For MCP / MCSE Certification:　　　　　　　　**Exam 70-270**
Installing, Configuring, and Administering Microsoft Windows XP Professional

ExamInsight For MCP / MCSE Certification:　　　　　　　　**Exam 70-290**
Managing and Maintaining a Microsoft Windows Server 2003 Environment

ExamInsight For MCP / MCSE Certification:　　　　　　　　**Exam 70-291**
Managing, and Maintaining a Microsoft Windows Server 2003 Network Infrastructure

ExamInsight For MCP / MCSE Certification:　　　　　　　　**Exam 70-292**
Managing and Maintaining a Microsoft Windows Server 2003
Environment for an MCSA Certified on Windows 2000

ExamInsight For MCP / MCSE Certification:　　　　　　　　**Exam 70-293**
Planning and Maintaining a Microsoft Windows Server 2003 Network Infrastructure

ExamInsight For MCP / MCSE Certification:　　　　　　　　**Exam 70-294**
Plan and Maintain a Microsoft Windows Server 2003 Active Directory Infrastructure

InsidersChoice to MCP / MCSE Certification:　　　　　　　　**Exam 70-296**
Planning, Implementing, and Maintaining a Microsoft Windows Server 2003
Environment for an MCSE Certified on Windows

ExamInsight For MCP / MCSE Certification:　　　　　　　　**Exam 70-297**
Designing Microsoft Windows Server 2003 Active Directory and Network Infrastructure

ExamInsight For MCP / MCSE Certification:　　　　　　　　**Exam 70-298**
Designing Security for a Microsoft Server 2003 Network:

InsidersChoice to MCP / MCSE Certification:　　　　　　　　**Exam 70-299**
Implementing and Administering Security in a Microsoft Windows Server 2003 Network

InsidersChoice: TotalRecall's Insiders Certification System Series:

InsidersChoice to MCP / MCSE Certification: **Exam 70-270**
Installing, Configuring, and Administering Microsoft Windows XP Professional

InsidersChoice to MCP / MCSE Certification: **Exam 70-290**
Managing and Maintaining a Microsoft Windows Server 2003 Environment

InsidersChoice to MCP / MCSE Certification: **Exam 70-291**
Managing, and Maintaining a Microsoft Windows Server 2003 Network Infrastructure

InsidersChoice to MCP / MCSE Certification: **Exam 70-292**
Managing and Maintaining a Microsoft Windows Server 2003
Environment for an MCSA Certified on Windows 2000

InsidersChoice to MCP / MCSE Certification: **Exam 70-293**
Planning and Maintaining a Microsoft Windows Server 2003 Network Infrastructure

InsidersChoice to MCP / MCSE Certification: **Exam 70-294**
Plan and Maintain a Microsoft Windows Server 2003 Active Directory Infrastructure

InsidersChoice to MCP / MCSE Certification: **Exam 70-296**
Planning, Implementing, and Maintaining a Microsoft Windows Server 2003
Environment for an MCSE Certified on Windows

InsidersChoice to MCP / MCSE Certification: **Exam 70-297**
Designing Microsoft Windows Server 2003 Active Directory and Network Infrastructure

InsidersChoice to MCP / MCSE Certification: **Exam 70-298**
Designing Security for a Microsoft Server 2003 Network

InsidersChoice to MCP / MCSE Certification: **Exam 70-299**
Implementing and Administering Security in a Microsoft Windows Server 2003 Network

ExamWise: TotalRecall IT Insight Certification Book Series:

ExamWise For MCP / MCSE Certification:	**Exam 70-210**
Managing Microsoft Windows 2000 Professional	
ExamWise For MCP / MCSE Certification:	**Exam 70-216**
Implementing and Administering a Microsoft Windows 2000 Network Infrastructure	
ExamWise For MCP / MCSE Certification:	**Exam 70-217**
Managing a Microsoft Directory Services Infrastructure	
ExamWise For MCP / MCSE Certification:	**Exam 70-219**
Designing a Windows 2000 Directory Services Infrastructure	
ExamWise For MCP / MCSE Certification:	**Exam 70-220**
Designing Security for a Microsoft Windows 2000 Network	
ExamWise For MCP / MCSE Certification:	**Exam 70-221**
Designing a Microsoft Windows 2000 Network Infrastructure	
ExamWise For MCP / MCSE Certification:	**Exam 70-227**
Installing, Configuring, and Administering Microsoft Internet Security and Acceleration (ISA) Server 2000, Enterprise Edition	
ExamWise For MCP / MCSE Certification:	**Exam 70-270**
Installing, Configuring, and Administering Microsoft Windows XP Professional	
ExamWise For MCP / MCSE Certification:	**Exam 70-290**
Managing and Maintaining a Microsoft Windows Server 2003 Environment	
ExamWise For MCP / MCSE Certification:	**Exam 70-291**
Managing, and Maintaining a Microsoft Windows Server 2003 Network Infrastructure	
ExamWise For MCP / MCSE Certification:	**Exam 70-292**
Managing and Maintaining a Microsoft Windows Server 2003 Environment for an MCSA Certified on Windows 2000	
ExamWise For MCP / MCSE Certification:	**Exam 70-293**
Planning and Maintaining a Microsoft Windows Server 2003 Network Infrastructure	
ExamWise For MCP / MCSE Certification:	**Exam 70-294**
Plan and Maintain a Microsoft Windows Server 2003 Active Directory Infrastructure	
ExamWise For MCP / MCSE Certification:	**Exam 70-296**
Planning, Implementing, and Maintaining a Microsoft Windows Server 2003 Environment for an MCSE Certified on Windows	
ExamWise For MCP / MCSE Certification:	**Exam 70-297**
Designing Microsoft Windows Server 2003 Active Directory and Network Infrastructure	
ExamWise For MCP / MCSE Certification:	**Exam 70-298**
Designing Security for a Microsoft Server 2003 Network	
ExamWise For MCP / MCSE Certification:	**Exam 70-299**
Implementing and Administering Security in a Microsoft Windows Server 2003 Network	

TotalRecall Certification Publications

CompTIA Titles

InsideScoop: TotalRecall's Complete Certification System Series:

InsideScoop to CompTIA A+ Hardware:	Exam 220-301
InsideScoop to CompTIA A+ OS:	Exam 220-302
InsideScoop to CompTIA Network+:	Exam N10-001
InsideScoop to CompTIA Security+ (Second Edition):	Exam SY0-101

InsidersChoice: TotalRecall IT Insight Certification Book Series:

InsidersChoice to CompTIA A+ Hardware:	Exam 220-301
InsidersChoice to CompTIA A+ OS:	Exam 220-302
InsidersChoice to CompTIA Network+:	Exam N10-001
InsidersChoice to CompTIA Security+: (Second Edition):	Exam SY0-001

ExamInsight: TotalRecall IT Insight Certification Book Series:

ExamInsight For CompTIA A+ Hardware:	Exam 220-301
ExamInsight For CompTIA A+ OS:	Exam 220-302
ExamInsight For CompTIA Network+:	Exam N10-001
ExamInsight For CompTIA Security+: (Second Edition):	Exam SY0-001

ExamWise: The TotalRecall Question Book Series:

ExamWise For CompTIA A+ Hardware:	Exam 220-301
ExamWise For CompTIA A+ OS:	Exam 220-302
ExamWise For CompTIA Network+:	Exam N10-001
ExamWise For CompTIA Security+ (Second Edition):	Exam SY0-101
ExamWise For CompTIA I-Net+ Certification:	Exam IK0-002
ExamWise For CompTIA Server+ Certification:	Exam SK0-001

Money Back Book Guarantee

This guarantee applies only to books published by TotalRecall Publications, Inc.! We are so confident in our products that we are prepared to offer the following guarantee to YOU, our valued customer: If you do not pass your certification exam after two attempts, we will give money back!

Visit http://www.totalrecallpress.com/

Select "Money Back Book Guarantee" for details.

Registered book purchasers who qualify will receive:

 1. 50% cash refund of purchase price

 2. free TotalRecall book of equal value

 NOTE: You must pay for shipping and handling.

To qualify for this TotalRecall Guarantee

you must meet these requirements and perform the following tasks:

 1. Register your purchase at the TotalRecall web site

  http://www.totalrecallpress.com/

 2. Fail the corresponding exam twice (No time Limit)

 3. Contact TotalRecall for the RMA # and to claim this guarantee

  Send email to **mailto:Guarantee@totalrecallpress.com**

  Subject must contain your Membership # or Registration #

Ship the following to claim your refund:

1. RMA # from returned email

2. Documents of exam scores for both failed attempts

3. Return the Book to the following address:

TotalRecall Publications, Inc.

Attn: Corby Tate

1103 Middlecreek

Friendswood, TX 77546

888-992-3131 **bfquiz@swbell.net**

281-992-3131

281-482-5390 Fax http://www.bfq.com/ or http://www.bfqd.com

It's a Passing day here at the BeachFront.

Thank you for using the TotalRecall Certification Success Program.

Bruce Moran, President

BeachFront Direct

**If you can PASS our Simulated Exam,
We Guaranty you will PASS the Real Exam.**

Call

888-992-3131

281-992-3131

**www.bfqd.com
www.BeachFrontDirect.com**

70-290 Download Instructions

BeachFront Quizzer (BFQ) version 4.0 Special Edition

System Requirements: Windows 95 & 98, Windows NT, XP Windows 2000 and Server 2003 with a minimum of 6 MB hard disk space and 16 MB RAM

The Center For Technology Certification, Inc. will help you accomplish your Microsoft Certifications. This state of art software program is designed to cut your study time in half, and get you to a passing level in the easiest and shortest amount of time possible. The program will adapt to you personally, and then lay out a prioritized study plan that will visually show you your progress on a day to day basis. When the software has recognized that you are at a passing level in each objective category, you're ready to sit for the exam! It's really that easy!!

Installation Instructions:

70-290 Practice Exam with eBook and Engine Download

1. Go to http://snipurl.com/SE70290 and download the practice exam ZIP file to a folder on your hard drive.
2. Open the WinZip file and Execute Quiz32.exe OR Execute SetupBFQ.bat to install the practice exam

This will install all software files:

4. Open the LicenseKey.txt file Copy and Insert the 12 digit number **License Key** when requested or type in the following License Key Numbers when requested.

TRP 70-290 SE Server 2003 Environment Special Edition = 368671665867

The software is very user friendly.
After you get the program installed Open Click on the Help button menu
Select contents for the on-screen manual. (You may want to print the Help File)
You will follow a six step process that will lead you through the program efficiently.
We are here to support you all the way. If you have any technical questions on the content, make sure you contact us. We are very proud of our pass rate, and we want you to contribute.

If you need additional assistance, visit our website www.totalrecallpress.com
Please let me know that the download and installation worked properly.
Thank you for purchasing our product and
Good Luck with your exam!

Sales:
    877-654-2265
    727-517-3694

Technical Support: info@bfq.com
    888-992-3131 or 281-992-3131
    Fax 281-482-5390

Made in the USA
Monee, IL
01 March 2026

45213754R00162